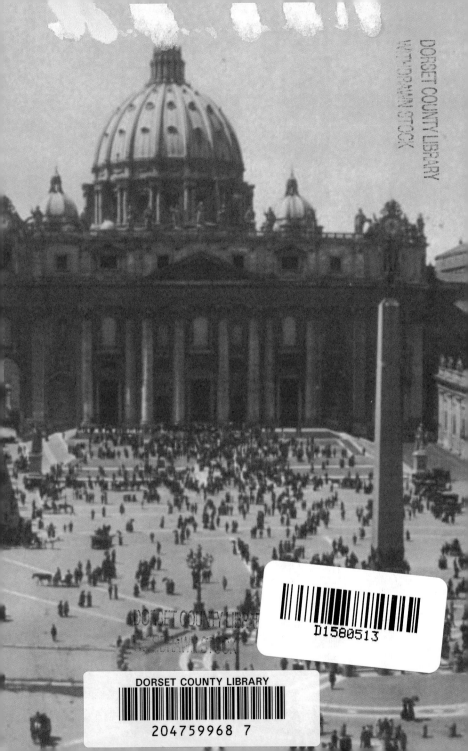

ST PETER'S

WONDERS OF THE WORLD

....

ST PETER'S

KEITH MILLER

PROFILE BOOKS

First published in Great Britain in 2007 by
Profile Books Ltd
3A Exmouth House
Pine Street
Exmouth Market
London ECIR OJH
www.profilebooks.com

1 3 5 7 9 10 8 6 4 2

Typeset in Caslon by MacGuru Ltd
info@macguru.org.uk
Designed by Peter Campbell
Printed and bound in Great Britain by
Clays, Bungay, Suffolk

The moral right of the author has been asserted.

A CIP catalogue record for this book is available from the British Library.

ISBN 978 1 86197 954 4

The paper this book is printed on is certified by the © 1996 Forest Stewardship Council A.C. (FSC). It is ancient-forest friendly. The printer holds FSC chain of custody SGS-COC-2061

FSC
Mixed Sources
Product group from well-managed
forests and other controlled sources
Cert no. SGS-COC-2061
www.fsc.org
© 1996 Forest Stewardship Council

For my late father, Reg Miller
ratiocinatio ac fabrica

CONTENTS

Now, let us make the fantastic assumption that Rome were not just a dwelling-place but a mental entity with just as long and varied a past history: that is, in which nothing once constructed had perished, and all the earlier stages of development had survived alongside the latest. This would mean that in Rome the palaces of the Caesars were still standing on the Palatine and the Septizonium of Septimius Severus was still towering up to its old height; that the beautiful statues were still standing in the colonnade of the Castle of St Angelo, as they were up to its sack by the Goths, and so on. But more still: where the Palazzo Cafarelli stands there would also be, without this being removed, the Temple of Jupiter Capitolinus, not merely in its latest form ... but also in its earliest shape, when it still wore an Etruscan design and was adorned with terracotta antefixae.

Sigmund Freud, *Civilisation and its Discontents*

FOREWORD

St Peter's Basilica in Rome is what people once unselfconsciously described as a great building. It is very old, very opulent and very, very large. Some of the most famous artists and architects in Western history have worked on or in it: Bramante, Raphael, Michelangelo, Bernini, Canova. It has been close to the heart of Western history for seventeen centuries. Like the great Gothic cathedrals, it is a building which is also a kind of city: the New Jerusalem, the City of God.

The first church on the site was part of a building spree undertaken by the convert emperor Constantine in the fourth century CE. At the core of the original St Peter's was a shrine constructed around the tomb where the bones of the saint were believed to lie. The shrine was preserved when one end of the fourth-century church was demolished to make way for a new and more elaborate replacement early in the sixteenth century. This decision was partly to do with the church's poor physical state after more than 1,000 years of use; but it also reflected the earthly ambitions of several of Peter's successors, the Popes: priests who were also kingmakers and princes.

The plan took a while to bear fruit, however. The surviving part of 'Old' St Peter's wasn't knocked down until the beginning of the seventeenth century, and 'New' St Peter's wasn't finished in anything like its present form until 1612, by which time the grand designs of a century before had given way to something more conventional, if still appropriately magnificent. As it stands, the building is a hybrid: a chimera or hippogriff. The dome, and the back and side parts of the exterior, are pretty close to Michelangelo's designs, hatched around the middle of the sixteenth century; the nave and main façade were done by Carlo Maderno in the early seventeenth century; the interior decoration and the great oval piazza in front of the church are by Bernini and date from the 1650s and 60s.

Soon after this long rebuilding, the ranks of pilgrims who had for centuries been thronging to Rome to honour Peter's remains began to be swelled by a new species of tourist. For these travellers – the phrase 'Grand Tourist' should probably only be applied to the wealthiest – the church was not so much a place of worship as a venue for education, an example of the rivalry between the 'ancients', the artists and builders of classical antiquity, and their 'modern' successors. These new responses to New St Peter's aimed towards a scholarly disinterest, though needless to say they were often skewed by the religious and political perspectives of the traveller. Because St Peter's was the biggest and most prestigious 'modern' building in a city dominated by the ruins of 'ancient' ones, it quickly became an eloquent barometer of European taste. Michelangelo's contributions were widely and consistently revered; Bernini was felt to have moved too far away from classical principles (not to mention a good few degrees too close to a certain strain of Roman Catholicism). Maderno was simply thought not to have been quite up to snuff. Nobody particularly troubled himself (or, much more rarely, herself) with the difficulties these three artists and their many colleagues must have encountered in trying to blend their works across more than a century (a century, come to that, which had seen the Catholic Church utterly transformed) – though it was generally conceded that the interior of the building, at least, was impressively harmonious.

This book will tell the story of a titanically ambitious architectural project, and try to evaluate the result. It will examine the ways in which St Peter's has been used to express the special relationship between imperial and papal authority, and how it has actually worked as a place of worship, pilgrimage, assembly and tourism at various points in its history. It will lay out the complex spatial and temporal dialogues entered into by the building, its many conversations with and appeals to other structures of every date and type across the uniquely eloquent Roman cityscape. It will peel back all the layers of rebuilding and disclose the few but telling remains of the old fourth-century basilica, and consider the enigma of the tombs beneath that. It will ask simple questions which architectural histories can sometimes overlook: what are churches for? What does it mean to imitate something? What is the relationship between a design on paper or in an artist's mind, and a concrete, realised thing? Is the self-assured 'greatness' of St Peter's nowadays nothing but an arrogant imposition which makes the modern visitor love and appreciate it less?

Although I hope it will be of interest and even use to travellers, this is not a travel guide. I have followed the path a visitor might take around St Peter's and stopped, as a visitor might, in front of architectural features and works of art which have interested me personally, and which I thought might shed some wider light on the building. I have not started at the beginning and worked my way through to the end, nor have I moved sequentially from the first chapel on the left to the last on the right. There are generalisations, digressions and ellipses in every dimension. I wanted to pass freely between descriptive and contextual elements – and to write a book which would be interesting to read. On pages xvi–xvii you will find a plan listing and locating the contents of the basilica. At the back of the book there are some notes on planning a visit to St Peter's, and a booklist for the curious or dissatisfied.

Translations are mine. Names of churches are anglicised where there is a widespread convention of doing so, as there is in the case of St John Lateran, but perhaps not of San Luigi dei Francesi or Santa Maria Maggiore. Measurements are given sparingly, and should anyway be taken with a generous pinch of salt. The fastidious terminology of classical architecture is used as little as possible. The quaint convention of describing parts of an occidented (i.e. west-facing) church like St Peter's as if it were a conventional, east-facing church will not be followed: in these pages, east is east, and west, correspondingly, west. I've also used what seemed like a commonsensical convention whereby the left- and right-hand sides of the basilica are apportioned from the viewpoint of the entrance, so the left aisle is on the south and the right on the north side.

One last thing. The history of the Vatican palace is intricately bound up with that of the church next door, but the two structures are largely and essentially separate. To give any kind of full consideration to the apartments, loggias, chapels, galleries, museums and gardens which make up the palace in a book this size would be impossible (the church alone is challenge enough). So I shall only be mentioning them when they bear on St Peter's in some direct way.

Keith Miller
London, 2007

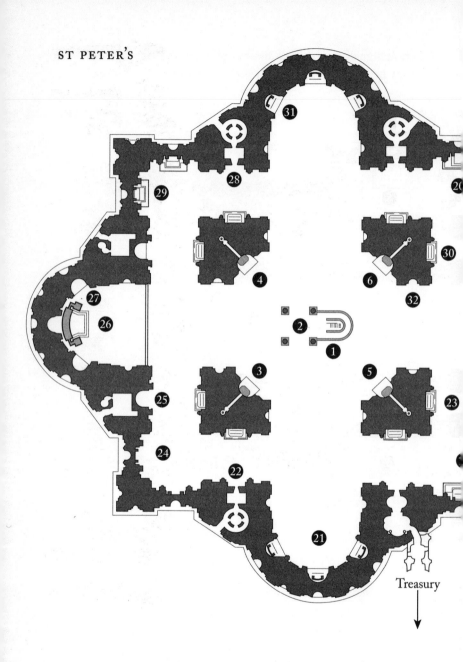

Treasury

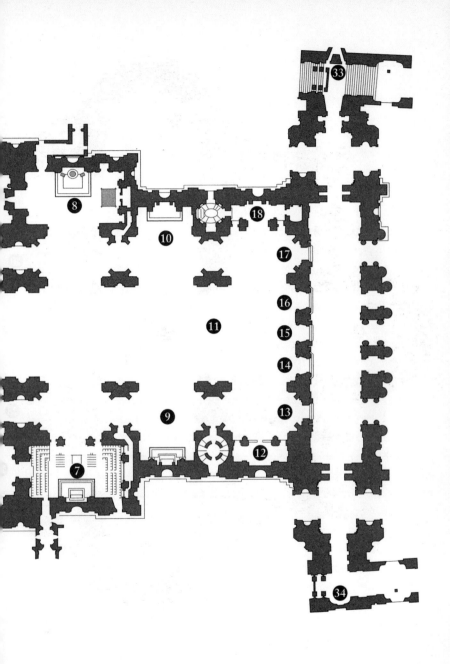

PLAN

Most things discussed in the text are located on the plan, as are the main mosaics and tombs. Undated mosaics are 18*c* after 17*c* originals.

1. Confessio, stairs by Maderno, icon 9*c*, pallium casket 18*c*.
2. Baldacchino by Bernini *et al.*, 1626–33. Altar of Clement VIII below. Above: dome by Michelangelo *et al.*, decorated with mosaics of saints, apostles, etc. after Cavaliere d'Arpino (early 17*c*).
3. Pier of St Veronica, statue by Mochi, 1629–40.
4. Pier of St Helena, statue by Bolgi, 1629–40.
5. Pier of St Andrew, statue by Duquesnoy, 1632–9.
6. Pier of St Longinus, statue by Bernini, 1635–8.
   (*Relics of all four of these saints are housed in a reliquary in the Pier of St Veronica. Mosaics of four evangelists in pendentives above crossing piers are by Giovanni de'Vecchi, late 16*c.)
7. Choir chapel, late 16*c*. The organ is apparently praiseworthy.
8. Chapel of the Most Holy Sacrament, late 16*c*, gate by Borromini (early 17*c*), ciborium by Bernini (mid-17*c*).
9. South aisle. Stuart memorial (1817) on south side of 1st pier from door; Innocent VIII's tomb by Pollaiuolo (15*c*) on south side of 2nd.

10. North aisle. Memorial to Queen Christina, by Carlo Fontana (turn of 18c) on pier nearest door.
11. Nave. Above the arches are sculptures of Virtues, by Bolgi, de' Rossi etc. *Rota* is in the centre, a few metres in from the Door of Filarete. Set into piers are busts of Popes, and statues of founders of Catholic orders, by followers of Bernini. Bernini's 6ft cherubs holding a holy water stoup on north side of 1st pier from door.
12. Baptistery chapel. Font is *c.* 10c, part of Emperor Otho II's tomb.
13. Door of Death, by Manzù.
14. Door of Good and Evil, by Minguzzi.
15. Door of Filarete. Reworked 17c mosaic of Giotto's *Navicella* (early 14c) is above, inside; *Feed My Sheep*, by school of Bernini above, outside.
16. Door of the Sacraments, by Venanzo Crocetti.
17. Holy door, by Vico Consorti.
    (*All doors mid-20c except Filarete's which is mid-15c.*)
18. Chapel of the Pietà, sculpture by Michelangelo (1499), vault by Lanfranco, mosaics after Pietro da Cortona.
19. Clementine chapel. Beneath the altar is Gregory the Great's tomb; next to it the tomb of Pius VII by Thorvaldsen.
20. Gregorian chapel. Opposite the altar is the tomb of Benedict XIV by Bracci.
21. South transept. Foreign-language confessionals. Mosaic of Peter's crucifixion after Reni on south-west altar.
22. Tomb of Alexander VII by Bernini and assistants, completed 1678.
23. Transfiguration, mosaic after Raphael's 16c original.
24. *Leo IV Repulsing Attila*, by Algardi, 17c.

25. Tomb of Paul III by Guglielmo della Porta, mid-16*c*.
26. Cathedra Petri, by Bernini, 1657–66. High altar is just in front.
27. Tomb of Urban VIII, by Bernini, completed 1647.
28. Tomb of Clement XIII by Canova, 1758–69.
29. Mosaic of St Petronilla after Guercino.
30. Mosaic of *Communion of St Jerome*, mosaic after Domenichino.
31. *Martyrdom* [in fact, evisceration] *of St Erasmus*, mosaic after Poussin.
32. Statue of St Peter, date and authorship uncertain, but traditionally given to Arnolfo di Cambio and so dated to the 14*c*.
33. Statue of Constantine, mid-17th century, by Bernini.
34. Statue of Charlemagne, early 18th century, by Cornacchini.

The collection displayed in the Treasury varies occasionally, but should include the Holy Column, one of the twisted columns which adorned the shrine of St Peter before the rebuilding of the basilica, believed on scant evidence to have been leant on by Christ; a ciborium by the Florentine sculptor Donatello from the 1430s; Pollaiuolo's monument to Sixtus IV, builder of the Sistine Chapel, from later in the same century; a terracotta model by Bernini of one of the angels flanking *his* ciborium in St Peter's; the papal tiara occasionally placed on the head of the bronze St Peter near the crossing of the basilica; various chalices, reliquaries, manuscripts etc.

APPROACHES

Taken as a walk not less than as a church, St Peter's of course reigns alone ... it serves where the Boulevards, where Piccadilly and Broadway fall short, and if it didn't offer to our use the grandest area in the world it would still offer the most diverting.

Henry James

A Roman summer morning is gathering its sultry forces outside. On most days the interior of the vast church is as cool as a wine-cellar; today the thousands packed into it have already generated a brow-mopping heat. Precisely at the appointed time, a curtain near the entrance to the church is drawn aside and a long line of clerics emerge. Sedately, the priests process down the long spine of the building towards the great well of space at its centre. One in particular attracts the attention of the crowd. There is a scrabbling for cameras, and a whisper of applause. The man's long robes hide shoes of a fabled elegance. He carries his predecessor's staff, crowned with a gnarled silver crucifix, its arms bowed by the weight of the suffering Christ. On his head is a bishop's mitre rather than the zeppelin-shaped tiara favoured by ancient tradition; the modesty implied by the choice will be lost on many who witness this event in person or on television.

The Pope, the Vicar of Christ, head of the Catholic Church and successor to Christ's follower Peter, presently reaches the heart of the church and sits on an elaborate throne set there for him. Prayers are said. The choir sings. There are readings, and a sermon, in which the Pope meditates on the nature of the job entrusted to Peter by Christ and asserts the direct, bodily link between Christ and the Christian: 'The Church in its heart is a community of the Eucharist.' The diplomatic side of his own job is revealed when he pronounces his hope that the Catholic and the Orthodox churches will one day unite, will 'drink together from the very Chalice, and eat together the Bread, which is the Lord Himself' (several high-ranking Orthodox officials and ecumenical think-tankers are present). His slow, clear Italian carries just a few hints of his native Germany – 'qvanto' for 'quanto' – but his homily wins a burst of applause even from people who haven't understood a single word of it.

Around an hour and a half into the ceremony, twenty-eight strips of white wool are brought to the Pope on several cushions. He drapes them around the shoulders of twenty-seven newly-appointed metropolitan bishops in turn, and then around those of the Archbishop Secretary of the Congregation of Bishops, who stands in for every other bishop in the Catholic world. Oaths are pronounced length-ily in Latin by each one.

By this time the crowd, or congregation, has grown rest-less. They have to hold their cameras above their heads and fire their zoom-lenses up to full strength if they are to have a hope of capturing the events taking place before the altar; the matter of direction is trusted to faith, unless a tall neigh-bour can be persuaded to press the button for them. Standing among them, one views the distant drama up ahead through a mosaic of illuminated screens, chaotic and intense. The event starts to seem like a strange hybrid: part rock festival, part speech day. After more singing and more praying comes a relatively rare occurrence, a papal Mass, during which Peter's successor performs for his colleagues (for now just the Catholic ones) the very ritual which he has been talking about: the Eucharist, the wine and wafers which believers believe really become the blood and body of Christ a moment or two before ingestion. Finally – not long before lunchtime – the Pope disappears down into a horseshoe-shaped void immediately below the altar before which he has sat all morning. Here he prays alone while the other assembled clergy file out in orderly striations of red and white. Outside, in a square which is not square but shaped like an enormous keyhole, a modest crowd of devoted Catholics and impatient tourists have gathered, keeping up with the ceremony inside on two enormous video screens.

The strips of cloth are called *pallia*, cloaks. They have spent the night in a silver casket at the spatial, historical and liturgical heart of St Peter's basilica, the largest Christian church in the world, as well as one of the oldest, in its foundation if not its fabric. They are made of lambs' wool which was itself blessed in another ancient church, Sant'Agnese, six months ago. Now they have inhaled another, wordless blessing from their night at the agreed burial-place of Peter himself, and today, the Festival of St Peter and St Paul, they are at last ready to be put – 'imposed' – over fifty-six episcopal shoulders. By this ritual, a spark of divine sanction is believed – by those who believe – to have passed from the first century CE directly to the year 2006, and to the present incumbent of this ancient office, Joseph Ratzinger, enthroned in 2005 as Pope Benedict XVI.

✠

There is an elegant phrase noted down in the archive of Fabio Chigi, who, as Pope Alexander VII, commissioned the last significant works to be carried out at St Peter's. It probably dates from the 1650s, and has often been attributed either to the Pope himself or to the basilica's then architect, the flamboyant Gian Lorenzo Bernini. 'The Church of St Peter,' it says, 'being, as it were, the model for all the others, will have to have a portico which can at once receive Catholics mother-like, with open arms, to confirm them in their belief: heretics, to reunite them with the church; and unbelievers, to light their way to the true faith.'

Quite a tall order for a portico. But the church of St Peter had, and to a degree retains, a sort of maternal status among Catholics (the Italian word I've translated as 'model' is *matrice*, which means 'womb' as well as 'model', 'mould' or 'template'). Confusingly, it isn't the *chiesa madre*, the mother church – that is St John Lateran, across town, where the Pope, in his secondary role of Bishop of Rome, has his *possesso*, his official seat. In fact the Vatican only became the main papal residence, and St Peter's next door the *de facto* papal church, in the fifteenth century. The status of the basilica derives from its history – founded by the convert emperor Constantine, or maybe his son Constans, to honour the tomb of Christ's apostle; richly stocked with relics; rebuilt and redecorated by the most famous artists in Italy. By the mid-seventeenth century, St Peter's had become the most important pilgrimage church in Europe. It would soon also loom large on the itinerary of even the least devout Grand Tourist, as Alexander VII well understood. It was the various needs, be they spiritual, emotional or aesthetic, of both tourist and pilgrim which Bernini's new portico, and the piazza framed by it, was to serve, and which, *mutatis mutandis*, it serves today.

In fact, the portico – a vague term denoting a covered, partly open space propped up by columns – does achieve a remarkable range of effects. It is two great arcs, each made up of four rows of gigantic travertine columns, with 140 stone saints writhing above them, all knitted together by two vast sickle-shaped entablatures which spring from either side of the church's wide façade. The complex piazza created by the portico, an oval joined on to a trapezium, is unquestionably one of the best-known and most spectacular urban spaces in the world. At times, at Easter, or on the festival of St Peter and St Paul, it can function as a huge, outdoor church; during the last illness of Pope John Paul II and the swift selection of his friend Joseph Ratzinger to succeed him, it witnessed extraordinary concentrations of passion and devotion. To the sceptic or agnostic, the aesthete, the tourist – the 'unbeliever' of the Codex Chigi – the piazza is scarcely less rewarding. The art lover will see in it an essay in Baroque architecture and urbanism which can hardly be bettered; the traveller will find distilled in it a quintessence of Rome and Italy. Like many grand urban spaces, it seems at first to be nothing but a celebration of itself. Well, you say to yourself as you pace out its shape or stand in its centre: here I am. On St Cecilia's day, 22 November 1786, Johann Wolfgang von Goethe and the artist Wilhelm Tischbein visited St Peter's. In his journal Goethe records how 'We walked up and down until we felt too hot, when we sat in the shade of the great obelisk – it was just wide enough for two – and ate some grapes we had bought nearby.' Ordinary human actions are elevated by such a setting to an almost ritualistic level. But in fact Piazza San Pietro serves many more specific purposes. It filters and processes arrivals to the church; it frames archetypal, endlessly reproduced views of St Peter's in one direction and the city of Rome in the other. Most of all it proclaims to visitors that they are crossing a boundary. It does this by means of a nuanced appeal to history and religious belief as well as the spatial drama which grips the senses more overtly.

The Piazza San Pietro was the last major element of the architectural complex at St Peter's to be built (it was finished in 1667), but it is usually the first thing visitors see. Faithful, heretic and unbeliever all arrive jumbled together: on foot along the Via del Conciliazione, a long boulevard, poker-straight and somewhat bombastic, designed by Marcello Piacentini in the 1930s and completed after the war; by metro, to Ottaviano-San Pietro station by the walls of the Vatican enclave a kilometre to the north, refurbished for the Jubilee in 2000 but already showing signs of wear and tear again; or packed like battery animals into the *speciale borseggiatori*, the 'pickpocket special', the number 64 bus from Termini railway station. Unlike most Italian piazzas, Piazza San Pietro has no pavement cafés, just a couple of news kiosks and, tucked away to one side, a stall selling rosaries and images of the Virgin, the late Pope, Padre Pio da Pietrelcina and other Catholic notables. The imposing space, with an obelisk looted from Egypt by the Roman emperor Caligula towering in the centre of it and two roaring fountains either side, is rarely empty of people, but has few of the distractions

– cars, shops and the rest – that you would expect to find in a conventional urban space, especially an Italian one. But it is important to remember that we are not in Italy any more. Romans who scurry across the piazza to send their letters by the fleetfooted Vatican post rather than its sluggardly Italian counterpart understand better than they would realise that this is a zone of transition, a soft but unmistakable boundary between a secular, democratic republic on one side, a scant 137 years old, and the rump of an ancient and granitically conservative theocracy on the other.

On 11 February 1929, Pope Pius XI signed a treaty with King Vittore Emmanuele III and his head of state, Benito Mussolini, recognising Italian sovereignty over what had been the Papal States. These had ceased to exist in practice nearly sixty years before, with the creation of a unified Italian state centred on Rome; but the papacy had been slow to concede its earthly powers in principle. Indeed it had been Pius's namesake Pius IX, who, having spent most of his long term of office battling against political reform, had initiated a policy of passive resistance against the Italian Occupation, as loyalist ultras continued to call the Risorgimento well into the twentieth century. With the treaty of 1929, the Pope's temporal dominions shrank to their present Ruritanian dimensions: St John Lateran, some churches and palaces in and around Rome and the citadel, palaces, churches and gardens on the Vatican hill. In return Italy gave the Pope 750 million lire in cash and bonds worth 5 million a year, and agreed that even if Church and State were to be formally separate, Catholic canon law would continue to form the basis for Italian legislation on marriage, divorce, abortion and so forth. The arrangement was renegotiated in the elegant decrepitude of Raphael's never-finished Villa Madama in 1984, but battles continue to be fought on these fronts today. One of the Italian Church's first actions after Benedict XVI's enthronement in May 2005 was to encourage Catholics to abstain from a referendum which sought to liberalise or secularise the law on various issues to do with assisted fertility and stem cell research.

The space between the 'arms' of Bernini's piazza is the only entirely open frontier between Italy and Vatican City. During the nervous days of the nineteenth century the piazza was often used for troop exercises, shows of strength by *ancien régime* allies in support of the threatened principle of papal sovereignty, the so-called 'temporal power'. Popular demonstrations tended to take place elsewhere, on the Capitoline or in the Piazza del Popolo (though the occupying French did celebrate a Festival of Federation in the Piazza San Pietro in 1798, even if this is best understood as a colonial rather than an emancipatory gesture; they built a catafalque to Napoleon's assassinated general Duphot there in the same year). Piazza San Pietro is not a Tiananmen or a Wenceslaus Square, a space which animates the citizen's sense of right or injustice. Visitors come to hear or see the Pope; or to hear news of the Pope. Its embrace is 'maternal' in this sense too: one is left in no doubt as to who is in charge.

The enormous area of the piazza in front of the church, and the gardens behind and beside it, make the Holy See not only the smallest state in the world, but also, peculiarly, one of the most spacious. The subtlety and dynamism of Bernini's design become apparent as you wander round the piazza. From the east, the Via della Conciliazione, it forms an ornamental frame for the basilica's façade. Once inside, the pedestrian does indeed feel some kind of embrace, a sense of enclosure in a grand, orderly system of rhythm and mass. The heftiness of the columns is offset by the parade of gesticulating saints above the entablature, dancing and frolicking just as the martyrologies insist they did at their earthly lives' end. From two marked-out viewpoints in the main, oval space, either side of the central obelisk, the fourfold colonnade itself becomes light and transparent, as the columns appear to fall into single file.

What Bernini was actually trying to accomplish with the piazza is not entirely clear, even if we accept that the quotation above is at least in accordance with his wishes and he wanted something which could make a direct emotional appeal to people, to beckon or hug. The complex form of the piazza, an ellipse combined with a trapezium, is more or less unique. Bernini's design shows his exceptional inventive powers, but it also reflects his awareness of other architects who had worked on the rebuilding of St Peter's over the previous century and a half. One modest influence may well have been the oval courtyard framing the *casino* of Pius IV, a little pleasure-house built in the Vatican gardens in the mid-sixteenth century by Pirro Ligorio, an antiquarian from Naples, whose architectural career had in many ways been a bit of a flop, but whose reconstructions of antique buildings were hugely influential well into the eighteenth century. Some sort of grand public space in front of St Peter's had been mooted since the 1450s, when the early Christian basilica was still standing. In 1586 Domenico Fontana, *il cavaliere della guglia*, the 'knight of the spire', moved the Vatican obelisk from its original position on the basilica's south flank to the large, but still formally untidy, piazza to the west, thereby giving the entrance to the basilica a grandiose, ceremonial quality it had previously lacked. Bernini's design would have to accommodate Fontana's obelisk, and a fountain installed in the piazza around the same time. It would also have to make the basilica's façade, one of the most criticised aspects of St Peter's, designed early in the seventeenth century by Fontana's nephew Carlo Maderno, look as good as possible.

Bernini's lodestar, though, will have been Michelangelo Buonarotti, architect of St Peter's from 1546 until his death in 1564. Later, we shall see how Bernini effaced almost every sign of Michelangelo from the inside of the church when he 'completed' its decoration at around the same time he was working on the piazza – though in this he was an agent of changing taste rather than the exacter of any sort of Oedipal vengeance. In the early 1640s he had already tried – and disastrously failed – to 'complete' Maderno's façade by putting twin bell-towers on either side of it. Michelangelo was dear to Bernini because his architecture had been informed by the deep understanding of the human body which he had acquired as a painter and sculptor. Bernini, another sculptor-architect, also made constant reference to the body as a template for architecture, not in the rigorous and abstract way we see in the sixteenth century, but in a pragmatic and almost lighthearted spirit. On his 1665 visit to France, he told his friend and host Paul Fréart de Chantelou that he had made the 'arms' of his colonnade at St Peter's smaller than the façade to make the 'shoulders' of the façade seem taller. He also told Fréart that just as stripes on a doublet make a small man seem taller, so columns on a building can have the same effect.

Bernini must have been acutely aware of one of

Michelangelo's most influential bits of architecture in Rome: the remodelling of the Campidoglio, the Capitoline hill, begun in his last years and finished off to his approximate specifications (just how approximate has been the subject of hot dispute, as at St Peter's) after his death. The site is pregnant with political and historical meaning. It was supposedly the first of the always rather ill-defined septet of hills to be settled by the ancient Romans, the site of their most important temple, the Capitolium, which loomed over what later became the Forum. In the Middle Ages it became the seat of the Senate, a shambolic and endlessly reorganised body scarcely worthy of its solemn, classicising name, which nevertheless at least sometimes stood up for the interests of the *commune*, the city of Rome, against the Popes. Cola di Rienzo (1313–54), the nearest thing Romans have to a popular hero, is commemorated on the Capitoline in a pointedly half-cocked way, with a bronze statue of only marginally more than garden-gnome size.

Michelangelo created a taut, trapezoid piazza between three buildings, one new, two adapted from existing ones. The shape's narrowest, open side faced north-west, away from the Forum; a broad flight of steps descending from this open edge created the impression of a terrace or parapet. The palazzi on either side were tilted inwards to frame a spectacular view of the Campus Martius, the flood-plain in the centre of Rome. The dome of St Peter's, already well under way when the work on the Capitoline was being done (and destined for completion at around the same time, the 1590s), was prominent on the horizon. In other words, the civic, secular rulers and administrators of the city would henceforward do their business within plain sight of their papal overlords across the river Tiber. This was a brilliant piece of scenography which may also have been an acute political statement (not something with which you'd readily credit Michelangelo, the romantic loner and republican sympathiser of legend). It was also an early example of an ongoing project by Rome's papal rulers to organise the city around dialogues or visual rhymes between one building or monument and another.

The tension and forcefulness of Michelangelo's trapezium, taking the orderliness and formal purity of the Renaissance tradition and tweaking it into something dramatic and even expressionistic, must have struck Bernini, nearly a century later, and must partly explain why he used it for the section of his piazza immediately adjacent to St Peter's itself. The two tapering wings either side of the façade (one of which contains an entrance to the Vatican palace) seem to lengthen slightly when seen from the threshold of the basilica, and to sharpen the edges of the two curving colonnades beyond. Bernini's design (Fig. 1) also creates a crook or cusp behind which the existing Vatican palace, which nestles untidily to the north and north-east of the basilica, could remain undisturbed. At least two rival designs from the seventeenth century called for a simple circular or elliptical piazza, much more in keeping than Bernini's solution with the classical tradition of elementary formal and geometrical consistency (and much more straightforwardly symbolic, representing in plan the orb of the earth topped with the roughly cross-shaped footprint of the basilica). But a round piazza of anything like the present size would have bitten off parts of the Vatican palace, so Bernini's compound form makes perfect practical sense.

Yet Bernini was also well aware of the monuments of classical antiquity – rather more so than his critics have tended

1. View of the Piazza San Pietro by Giovanni Battista Piranesi, from *Vedute di Roma*, mid-eighteenth century. Piranesi was an almost uniquely skilled etcher, and his prints are full of contrasting textures, varying widths of line and almost abstract rhythmic effects. Here the crisp lines of the architecture contrast with the feathery background and the churned-up foreground. This view is skewed to emphasise the Apostolic Palace of the Vatican, the boxy building just right of centre.

to paint him. As we shall see, St Peter's is full of complex and subtle responses to the rich architectural legacy of ancient Rome. These may be acts of homage and filiation, or something more competitive and even antagonistic. The church's constituent forms – circles, squares, hemispheres – and structures – stone columns, arches and pediments, concrete vaults, domes, marble facings – are derived not only from the classical Roman tradition in general, but from identifiable Roman buildings in particular. It would be odd if the piazza which completes and heralds the basilica itself were exempt from this ongoing dialogue with the past.

One possible prototype is particularly intriguing. References to the Piazza San Pietro from the seventeenth and eighteenth centuries often call it a *teatro* or *anfiteatro*. This must mean more than an early acknowledgement of the sense of display which the space confers on those who move through it (which Goethe clearly appreciated, and which both cassocked clerics and linen-suited laity continue to exhibit today). In fact, it is a reference to the Roman forms which Bernini's two curved colonnades indirectly evoke. The theatre was a Greek invention, of course; doubling the semicircular form of the theatre to create the amphitheatre (the prefix *amphi-* meaning 'on both sides') was Rome's contribution to the history of entertainment. The amphitheatre was a defining characteristic of Roman society: a sort of inversion of the Roman world, with the periphery brought into the centre and theatricalised, in the form of parades of exotic animals dragged through the arena, criminals put to death during slack moments, and slaves and prisoners-of-war made to fight each other with nets, spears or the ever-popular *gladius*, or short stabbing sword – whence 'gladiator'.

The amphitheatre became a particularly tainted institution for the early Christians. It is not quite clear how many people were actually put to death in the arenas of the Roman world, never mind how many Christians. Martyrdom being a cherished vocation for adherents to this curious new religion, and the wickedness of pagan Rome being something which they lost no opportunity to decry, accounts written by Christians are doubly untrustworthy. But the sensibilities of good Christians were anyway outraged by the barbarism that was gladiatorial combat, whoever was on the bill. Augustine laments in the *Confessions* how his friend Alypius fell in with a fast crowd in Rome, and soon became hooked on the sanguinary spectacle of the games: 'When he saw the blood, it was as if he had drunk madness.' The episode is a good example of the complex entanglement of Christian beliefs and practices with pagan ones in the fourth century; we shall see plenty more evidence of this in, or rather beneath, St Peter's.

All in all, the form of a Roman amphitheatre seems an unlikely one to find commemorated in a Christian building, much less the most important church in Christendom. But to say so is to disregard the elementary convention of appropriation, widely used in ecclesiastical architecture, whereby building something out of materials salvaged from something else, or on top of something else, or in the form of something else, is intended to convey a sense of having withstood or overcome that something. Indeed the Colosseum itself, the largest and most prestigious amphitheatre in the Roman world, was consecrated in 1675 and dedicated to St Mary of the Martyrs. Carlo Fontana put a design forward to 'restore' it, with a new, frescoed loggia and a little elliptical church nestling inside, which might have been charming, but was passed over in favour of the simpler solution of a cross and a dedicatory inscription fixed in the ruins.

During the Renaissance, the Colosseum had been used by architects in a more precise way, as a model of how Roman builders had used an effect of columns in relief to make an arcade structurally strong and visually interesting. Its distinctive rhythm was imitated on buildings in Rome, Florence and elsewhere. There is no such literal imitation in the Piazza San Pietro. But the elliptical space created by Bernini's colonnade is certainly not unlike a simplified and idealised amphitheatre. Bernini even intended a 'third arm', closing the ellipse off from the east, which would have made its elliptical shape even clearer. Meanwhile, the stone saints lining the roof of the colonnade mean that, among other things, we are to read the piazza as a place which honours martyred Christians – both the legendary early victims of the Roman terror and, by implication, more recent casualties in the East and the New World. The jaunty postures of the saints above the colonnade now begin to make more sense. The blowsy sensuality of Bernini's sculpture has come in for plenty of criticism since his death, but these statues – done in his style, if not by his hand or necessarily to his precise designs – strive after an effect of insouciance and ecstatic transfiguration. The quality of lightness conferred – with varying degrees of success, it has to be allowed, though the figures need only ever be seen from a distance – on the figures suggests the saints' weightless souls, freed from the body, ascending gleefully to heaven. It is worth pointing out that the temporary structures erected inside the basilica to celebrate the canonisation of new saints were also called *teatri*.

So the piazza is a metaphysical threshold as well as a peculiarly quaint national one. Most of the thousands of visitors who come to St Peter's on an ordinary day will scarcely notice the saints ringed round above their heads – if they do, it will be for their formal or compositional qualities, the way they relieve the heaviness of Bernini's entablature, even (in what must be the most marked change of taste since the seventeenth century) their vividly coarse detailing. Nor will the devout have much time for them, tastes in religious art having changed a little too. But in fact they are a welcoming committee, greeting the thousands of new visitors who tumble, thirsty and expectant, into the great piazza every day, drawing them in, offering them a hinted lesson on what the gigantic building at the piazza's western edge is actually for.

⧖

At present an airport-style security screen is in operation at St Peter's, tucked away under the north colonnade. Visitors pass through metal-detectors and submit their bags to the scrutiny of X-ray scanners. This also allows any shortcomings in the matter of dress to be corrected, shorts and vests being firmly prohibited inside the basilica. The visitor is eventually restored to the trapezoid part of the piazza, just in front of the church. Statues of St Peter and St Paul frame the approach to the façade. The ensemble is wide, serene and, since the 2000 restorations, surgically clean. Here it may be natural to turn away from St Peter's itself and take one more look back at the piazza: the great obelisk, the roaring, iridescent fountains (the one on the south side is Bernini's copy of the one on the north, which was installed a few feet from its present position by Maderno in 1613; together, they form a pleasing dialogue with Piacentini's twin 'propylaea', two blocky buildings framing the neck of the Via della Conciliazione and the view back towards the Castel Sant'Angelo and the river). Then it will be time to swivel round again, and examine the church whose enormous façade rears overhead.

The man who got to sign St Peter's was neither artist nor architect, but the Pope who oversaw its completion, Paul V. The inscription which runs across the entablature commemorates the papal deed in the usual Latin:

IN HONOREM PRINCIPIS APOST PAULUS V
BURGESIUS ROMANUS PONT. MAX. AN. MDCXII
PONT. VII.

Paul V Borghese, the Roman, Pope, [did this] in honour of the prince of Apostles in the year 1612, the seventh of his papacy. Both Paul's title and that of his illustrious predecessor St Peter come from Roman antiquity: *princeps* is one word for 'emperor', while *pontifex maximus* means 'High' or 'Chief Priest', a political as well as a religious office.

The central mass of the façade is crowned with the crucial thing: Paul's family name and the assertion that he was a Roman, not a Florentine – though his father was Sienese – a Neapolitan or who knew what. The *stemma*, the family crest, appears below the name: an eagle (another old imperial symbol) and a dragon. *Burgesius* or Borghese is cognate with *borgo*, an archaic term for 'town'; in Rome it was long used to describe the district west of St Peter's, over which the Popes traditionally exercised direct, feudal control. With this seemingly curt inscription Paul emphasises the localising aspects of his papacy, his paternal care of his townsmen. What is more, as their ruler, he was responsible for their bodily well-being as well as the care of their souls. From the Janiculum hill, south of St Peter's, two of Paul's *grands projets* are visible. To the left stands the rebuilt basilica, Michelangelo's dome atop Maderno's nave. To the right, seen from nearby and thus looking about the same size as the vastly larger church at the bottom of the hill, a fountain built under Paul V and dubbed the Acqua Paola. The symmetry between church and fountain isn't just an accident of perspective. Four redundant columns from the nave of Old St Peter's, demolished on Paul's orders, were thriftily and significantly incorporated into the new papal fountain. In restoring the antique aqueducts and bringing clean water into the city, Paul and his predecessor Sixtus V (born Felice Peretti, whence the name Acqua Felice or 'happy water' which was used to describe his fountain on the Quirinal hill) were consciously reviving the old imperial duty of *munificentia*, the ruler's generosity to the ruled, just as the papal government perpetuated old Roman policies like the *horrea* or public granaries. The Acqua Paola was to be an ornament in the earthly life of Rome, just as the new basilica would enhance its spiritual life.

Borghese also means bourgeois, a resonance which means rather more now than it did then. Not that Borghese was bourgeois, of course, any more than the artist Louise Bourgeois is bourgeois today. But the word's connotations of pomposity and dullness are ironic to say the least, given that these are two failings which have been widely identified in the façade of St Peter's. Yet as one stands before the church, some of the conventional objections levelled at Maderno's work seem a little unfair. The heavy attic, a strip of horizontal mouldings running all the way across from one side to the other, seems expressive and powerful rather than anodyne. The statues of Christ and the apostles placed along the top of the façade animate it in very much the same way as the saints do the piazza. The triangular pediment seems bolder, and less submerged in the whole, than it does from a couple of hundred metres away. The uncertain relationship between the façade and the dome is hardly a problem, as the dome is hidden behind the height of the building. The rich decoration underneath the famous benediction loggia, the heavy Michelangelesque ornament surrounding the attic windows and the effervescent eighteenth-century clocks in the upper corners all give the eye something to do, while the sheer mass of the façade duly impresses and overwhelms. After noon, there is a tiny dividend of sensual pleasure; a cast shadow slowly deepens in front of the church, bringing with it a smell of cooling hot stone and dust, offering a promise of relief from the Roman sun, leading the way in to the deeper shadows inside.

But the steps immediately in front of St Peter's are also a good spot from which to start to map out and measure this imposing, overwhelming building. You will notice how much the piazza slopes down from north to south (left to right if you have your back to the church). The two arches piercing the ends of the façade are of considerably different depths. There are more steps separating the church from the piazza on the downhill than the uphill side. You may spot the fact that the southern wing, where the ticket office and souvenir shop are, is bent more sharply inward than its ostensible twin on the northward, or Vatican, side. This is a curious sort of perfection ('There are a hundred errors in St Peter's,' Bernini said).

Just as the bones of St Peter form the kernel of everything which has since been built around them on the site, so Peter himself was the foundation of organised Christianity. *Tu es petrus*, Christ told him as he handed him the keys of heaven, *et super hanc petram aedificabo ecclesiam meam*. The words are written in Latin and Greek around the gilded frieze inside St Peter's. *Petros* means 'rock' in Greek, and, so by adoption, does *petra* in Latin; Christ is punningly telling Peter that he is the rock on which the Christian Church will be built. Peter, the horny-handed fisherman recruited on the Sea of Galilee, isn't quite convincing as management material. When he denies Christ three times in one night, or prepares to flee Rome before seeing an apparition of Christ on the Appian Way and being almost shamed into martyrdom, he seems like an attractively flawed, human figure. Certainly he's not the only disciple to receive the fire of the Holy Spirit at Pentecost after the Crucifixion, when he and the other disciples are charged with spreading the word across the world, and equipped with the power to speak in different languages in order to do so. But he is the only one to receive this particular commission. Christ explicitly places Peter at the head of the new Church. Peter will be the vicar of Christ, and will retrospectively be regarded as the first Pope. Every other head of the Roman Church, right down to Joseph Ratzinger, is said to join this chain of divine authority, a metempsychotic or even shamanic transference whereby there is a little splinter of Peter in every Pope, and, through Peter, a little splinter of Christ.

It is ironic, therefore, that Peter's church is not founded on a rock, but on sludgy alluvial soil. The north-western half of the building, the lower slope of the Vatican hill, has secure foundations dug into bedrock; the south-eastern half does not. Ever since a church was first built here in the fourth century CE, this has been a problem. The heavy columns lining the nave of Old St Peter's rested on massive brick, stone and concrete walls which ran at intervals beneath it. These also help to sustain the new church (though the really heavy and potentially unstable part, the dome, is on surer ground than the nave). This is why the first serious attempt to rebuild the church failed in the early sixteenth century; this is why Bernini's bell-tower started to collapse soon after he started building it in the mid-seventeenth. It is also why the heavy footings of the Circus of Gaius and Nero, a first-century race-track which used to be where the southern edge of St Peter's is now, were retained and used to fix the foundations, not only of Constantine's basilica, but also the rebuilt version. This is – probably – why the great obelisk in the piazza is not quite in line with the central axis of the church, as it now seems Fontana used the edge of the Circus as a foundation for his transplanted obelisk (originally it had – probably – stood halfway along the central *spina*, or ridge), and the Circus was not quite aligned or to scale with the church.

It was the much-maligned Maderno who ensured that you can only notice the misplacement of the obelisk from a couple of places: either the eastern edge of the piazza, where you will see that the dome, the centre of the façade and the obelisk never quite line up, or inside the church, along the central axis of the nave, where a glance out through the main door reveals the obelisk standing unmistakably left of centre (it's around four metres to the north). He did this by tilting the façade a couple of degrees anticlockwise, so the loggia which separates the church from the outside world is a little wider on its southern than its northern edge. Nothing one can easily spot, though accurate ground-plans of the basilica and piazza can look a little wobbly to the careful observer. Unsurprisingly, Maderno has never received much credit for this sleight of hand. Francesco Milizia, a leading light of Italian neoclassicism in the late eighteenth century, and a bitter opponent of the baroque style inaugurated by Maderno and his contemporaries, said he'd got muddled (*imbrogliato*) among the ruins of the old basilica.

This sort of pedantry is typical of interested parties down the ages, and the layperson may be forgiven for asking what all the fuss is about. The answer is that St Peter's is a building with an immensely long and convoluted building history, but one which nonetheless presents the visitor with an uncannily synthetic appearance. It has been scrupulously maintained and continuously restored (compare the experience of stumbling into a neglected and dilapidated Baroque gem off some flyblown backstreet in Naples, say, where the peeling stucco ornament seems arrested in a process of growth as much as of decay). Beneath the even, glassy surfaces of the church, it is not always easy to tease apart the various ideas and fashions which have influenced the different stages of its construction (again, compare a church like St John Lateran, with its Gothic cloister and baldacchino, Byzantine mosaics, Renaissance ceiling, Baroque nave and Early Christian baptistery, all of which are bracingly indifferent to each other). So looking for inconsistencies and imperfections in St Peter's – Bernini's 'hundred errors' – isn't just malicious nit-picking. It helps you to understand the building. Something which has been buffed to within an inch of its life does not readily give up its secrets. Spotting the chinks in the basilica's armour – the spongy, impractical site on which it was built, and the various consequences that has had, for a start – allow the visitor to engage with it more attentively, in a spirit of something other than mere passive stupefaction. Quite apart from anything else, these days we tend to be more attracted to something which has a few flaws.

So, pilgrim or aesthete, zealot or sceptic, all should take heart and courage on the threshold of this mother of all churches. It is huge, it is bewildering, it is immaculate, and it is relentless. In the sense understood by the twenty-first century, few would call it a 'beautiful' building. But behind the great basilica's polished surfaces and awesome dimensions lie other buildings, begun and dismantled, or only dreamed of, here; or built, used and lost elsewhere. A church is both a tool and a symbol (even a symbol is a kind of tool, Wittgenstein said); and St Peter's is, despite everything, the greatest church in the world.

....

2

PRIESTS AND PRINCES

How many divisions has the Pope?

Josef Stalin (attrib.)

Once under the loggia and through the doors – there are five doorways, though one turns out, confusingly, to be walled up on the inside – visitors to St Peter's soon begin to segregate. The devout and repentant, the halt and the lame begin a systematic round of altars and reliquaries, or head for the confession booths. Most tourists join a torrent of artistic pilgrims rushing to admire Michelangelo's *Pietà*, one of the most celebrated works of Italian High Renaissance art, now tucked safely behind glass in the first chapel on the north aisle as if it were a star exhibit in an aquarium, or a witness in a Mafia maxi-trial. St Peter's is packed with works of art, though the Michelangelo is very much the best-known. In fact, the doors themselves are a series of works of art, enriched with relief sculptures in bronze. The oldest are Renaissance, from the 1440s, transplanted from Old St Peter's; the newest, which commemorate the controversial Second Vatican Council in 1962–5, are among a handful of twentieth-century contributions to the rebuilt basilica. Even here, just at the mouth of the leviathan, there is no shortage of details to catch the eye. But without wishing to deny Michelangelo his celebrity as a sculptor, it may be better to disregard the *Pietà* for now, to ignore the intricate bronze doors, instead to take a few seconds just to breathe in the unique vastness of the space, fully 186 metres from door to apse: to try to get to grips with the interior of the basilica as a whole.

The impact of the church, from the piazza and the façade to the outsized, opulent interior, gathers into a massive crescendo of opulence, power and grandeur. The combined effects of scale, space, richness of materials and elaboration of ornament seen and felt at St Peter's are more potent than in any other building, religious or secular, anywhere in the world. To be sure, this has something to do with glorifying God. It also has something to do with the saint purportedly buried at the church's heart. But the strongest impression one gets is of worldly power and worldly wealth. To find out why, we must disregard for a moment the magnificent pile standing so proudly round us and think about its predecessor, the basilica built by a convert emperor in the fourth century CE. We must also begin to think about the peculiar status of the Popes, and the shrewd way in which they learned to buttress their spiritual authority against the military and political clout of the rulers of Europe, becoming, five centuries or so after Constantine, princes in their own right.

So just what is a 'basilica', anyway? The short answer is: an oblong church with a high space running along the centre of its longer axis – a 'nave' – flanked by lower aisles or chapels. By that definition, St Peter's, with its high dome and humpbacked shape, ought not to qualify. But the church we see today is, as we have said, a peculiar kind of shrine or reliquary, not only to the saints incorporated within it, but also to the previous incarnation of its own architectural self.

It is usually called a basilica not because of what it is, but what it was.

Before the Christianisation of Rome, the basilica was a secular building, a venue for public assembly and – conventionally – legal trials. It is probably best not to read too much into the early Christians' adoption of the form after Constantine legitimised the religion in 313 CE. To be sure, the standard-issue basilica was a spacious and imposing building, and its division into a great central space and more intimate marginal ones meant that different rituals could all take place at the same time. Another obvious candidate for appropriation, the pagan temple, was ill-adapted to Christian worship, which was more about congregating inside a building than milling around outside it. What is more, most pagan temples still had pagans in them at this point. So the basilica must have been a largely pragmatic choice. But still, taking an architectural form which gave concrete expression to the political and legal heft of the Roman State and dedicating it to a god only just taken off the proscribed list was also a perfect demonstration of Christianity's new authority. A gentle thumbing of the nose at the old pagan oppressor might now have seemed in order even to the saintliest – though, of course, Jesus himself had taken a conciliatory line on the issue, exhorting the faithful to render unto Caesar that which was Caesar's.

The interesting thing about Christianity in the early fourth century is that when Constantine made the religion not only lawful, but, by adopting it himself, fashionable, the infamous persecutions of Diocletian lay just a scant decade in the past (it's as if the next US president after George W. Bush were to convert to Islam). Constantine was the son of

Constantius, one of three co-rulers appointed by Diocletian between 286 and 293 CE to form a fragile governing entity known as the Tetrarchy, or rule of four. In 306, Constantine was hailed as Emperor by the army at York – Geoffrey of Monmouth thought his grandfather was Old King Cole, incidentally – and the Tetrarchy quickly unravelled into civil war. Eusebius's nearly contemporary *Life of Constantine* says that the would-be emperor had a vision before he was to fight his rival Maxentius at Milvian Bridge, just north of Rome, in late October of 312 CE. A fiery cross, or perhaps a Chi-Rho, a Greek pictogram representing the first two letters of Christ's name which became a popular Christian symbol around this time, appeared in the sky before Constantine. *En tout i nika,* or *In hoc signo vinces,* said a voice – by this sign you'll be victorious. Convert and you will prevail over Maxentius. Sure enough, he did, and he did; and the Edict of Milan, freeing Christians to worship as they wished, and restoring any confiscated goods to them, followed in 313.

Even after his alleged vision, Constantine was not a deeply committed Christian in any sense we would recognise – and Roman Christianity retained a passing resemblance to paganism. Constantine had previously shown a conspicuous interest in the cult of Apollo (a vision of the god not unlike his later vision at Milvian Bridge is recorded). An image uncovered in one of the tombs underneath St Peter's seems to be from around the time of Constantine, and depicts Christ as Sol, an avatar of Apollo, the charioteer of the sun (see Chapter 5). There is a line in an early martyrology which may say 'God alone' – *soli* – or 'the god Sol' – *solis.* The exquisite round mausoleum of Constantine's daughter Constantia, attached to the mostly lost basilica of St Agnes on Via Nomentana just east of Rome, is girt round with fourth-century mosaics in which the winemaking imagery traditionally associated with the god Bacchus (and extremely common in pagan funerary art) is co-opted to evoke the Christian eucharist, the ritualised assimilation of the body and blood of Christ. Constantine's triumphal arch, a spectacular bricolage of earlier sculptures near the Colosseum, makes a grudging reference to *divinitas* – 'the deity' – in its dedicatory inscription, but is otherwise indistinguishable from a pagan monument. Eight years after the Edict of Milan, the Emperor confirmed a Christian sabbath – *dies Solis*, again confusingly implying a still-pagan Sunday rather than the Son-as-in-Son-of-God glossed by later Christian commentators. The same year he issued a decree confirming the privileges of the *haruspices*, practitioners of an ancient Etruscan technique whereby the liver of a sacrificed animal is sliced open to predict the future.

Roman society had always been aggressively monocultural in some ways, and attractively laissez-faire in others. Provided only that the supremacy of the state and the divinity – in the fairly elastic sense that the Romans understood that term – of the Emperor be acknowledged, people could support the cult of Mithras or Isis – though both these cults became controversial themselves – and adopt whomever they liked as their lares or domestic deities. A house in Pompeii has even yielded up a little ivory statue of the Hindu goddess Laksmi, though this may have been a traveller's token rather than the object of even the rather low-octane worship conducted at the household shrine. Monotheism, of course, was quite another matter. Many Christians refused to sacrifice to the Emperor, thereby compelling their own martyrdom – or even sought to compel their own martyrdom by refusing to sacrifice to the Emperor. A famous pair of letters exchanged by Pliny the Younger and Trajan early in the second century CE clearly shows both Romans bending over backwards to reach some workable compromise, Trajan in particular urging restraint, and ordering Pliny not to give way to police-state tactics (Pliny says that whatever these people have or haven't done, their *pertinacia* – a quasi-legal term meaning something a little like our contempt of court – ought to be punished).

Christian antagonism towards Roman identity and the Roman State tended to increase over the century or so leading up to Milan. Christ's render-unto-Caesar policy gave way to something more implacable, as when Origen advised Christians not to serve in the military in the third century CE. During this period some wealthy and prominent Romans did embrace Christianity, of course. The clause in the Edict of Milan – or the 'rescript', or form letter summarising its contents which Eusebius quotes in his *History of the Church* – about restoring their goods to Christians only makes sense if there were goods to restore at the time. But before Milan, Christian ritual had largely taken place in modest, domestic settings. It had not been necessary nor, even allowing that persecution was probably the exception rather than the rule, desirable, for the Christians to evolve a monumental architecture of their own. In 313, the secular form of the basilica was a pragmatic choice. Without too much tinkering, it would serve the Christians of the Empire as cemetery, reliquary, treasury and meeting-house, all in one.

Constantine himself funded the first large Christian basilicas to appear in Rome. Old St Peter's was probably built during the 320s and 30s (the traditional date for its consecration, 326, is almost certainly wrong, and recent commentators even go so far as to suggest that the basilica was completed or even initiated not by Constantine at all, but by his son Constans). It took the form of a high T-shaped central space made up of a nave and two simple transepts, two aisles on each side of the nave and a semicircular niche or apse set into the western wall. Early Christian sources testify to the richness of its decoration; a fourth-century martyr poem by Prudentius calls it *aurea tecta*, a golden building, and talks about the baptistery beside the church as if it were some kind of magical grotto. Dale Kinney has written about the rich marble columns, taken from earlier buildings, which lined the nave. The basilica, together with six others (seven being the legendary number of hills in Rome, the figure had a pleasing symmetry, as well, perhaps, as a pungent little kick of religious symbolism), rapidly grew into a draw for pilgrims second only to Jerusalem itself.

It is difficult to see anything much like Old St Peter's in Rome today, though drawings of the building survive from various periods. Most early Christian churches are variations on the basilica template, but generally much smaller than the big imperial projects. Many early churches of whatever size will also have been redecorated in later periods with frescoes, stucco or marble ornament, relief sculptures, wooden roofs and so on. Whether this later decoration survives or not – and if it doesn't it will probably have been chiselled off in the early twentieth century – the result will be equally remote from the church's original appearance. The best option may be to pay a call on the vast basilica of San Paolo fuori le Mura on Via Ostiense to the south of the city. This was lavishly and fussily restored after a fire in the nineteenth century, and so looks a little off-the-peg; the mosaics might be more at home

Obeliscus Vaticanus

2. Late sixteenth-century engraving showing the eastern half of Old
St Peter's, with the Vatican obelisk in its original position on the south
side. The church is largely hidden by the baptistery and the chapel of St
Petronilla, either side of the obelisk. One version of Bramante's design for
rebuilding the church had it orientated to the south, with the main entrance
squared up to face the obelisk (an imposing spatial and axial marker which
also stood near one possible site of Peter's martyrdom).

[32]

lining the walls of a cinema (Augustus Hare said the church looked like a railway station). But the large scale, the high, central tunnel of space, the classical columns, double aisles and glimmering decoration are not unlike surviving images of the first church of St Peter's. The scruples which many cognoscenti feel about over-restoration should not blind us to the fact that San Paolo fuori le Mura probably has more in common with its fourth-century self than 'purged' churches of similar antiquity which came to the antiquarians' notice in the different, but in its way no less aggressive, climate of the early twentieth century. It suits the antiquarian – and, for different reasons, the believer – to ascribe a primitive purity and restraint to ancient, unspoilt places of worship, but there is no evidence that Rome's early Christians much liked whitewash or bare brickwork, even before Milan.

Peter and Paul are often paired up in Christian art: Prudentius compares them to a new Romulus and Remus, and even says they were martyred on the same day a year apart (they still have a joint festival, 29 June – see Chapter 1). The Acts of the Apostles make it clear that they are the most imposing figures in the new church. Paul's letters give early Christianity its character to a greater extent than any other single body of writing (riding roughshod over what Jesus himself taught, it has been argued), and Peter founded three of what soon became known as archbishoprics: at Jerusalem, Antioch and Rome. That the third office soon became synonymous with leadership of the entire Church was partly a function of Rome's special status as *caput mundi*, the head of the world, and partly with Peter's pre-eminence among Christ's disciples. *Tu es Petrus,* remember; Peter is the foundation of the Church, and the gatekeeper of Heaven. Indeed, the second part of Peter's job description has led to innumerable cartoons, jokes and sketches in which this or that famous decedent has an altercation with Peter outside the proverbial Pearly Gates, the apostle's keys jangling janitorially in his belt, a nightclub bouncer's clipboard in his hand. One dialogue dating back to the early sixteenth century, and once attributed to Erasmus, sets Pope Julius II at loggerheads with his predecessor; another takes the architect Bramante to task for having played fast and loose with Peter's basilica (see Chapter 3).

Paul, a Roman citizen (and former soldier), was given a citizen's death, decapitation with a sword. Fountains sprang up where his head bounced on the floor, a good example of the peculiar gaiety which attends scenes of martyrdom in early Christian writings. There's a church on the supposed site of Paul's martyrdom, the Tre Fontane south of Rome. By the time of Constantine, his body had apparently been moved at least once, to San Sebastiano (which served as a sort of holding pen for martyrs' corpses during the second and third centuries) on the nearby Appian Way. It was duly moved again, to San Paolo fuori le Mura, where it still supposedly abides.

Peter had a rougher time of it. One source says he was crucified – this being the slave or non-citizen's death – *inter duas metas,* between two cones or pyramids. The precise definition of *meta* is difficult to be sure about. It is used to describe the large structures, somewhat resembling attenuated blancmanges, which marked the turning points in a Roman racetrack. It is also applied more generically to structures of that sort of shape – the *meta sudans* or 'sweaty hillock' was a famous fountain near the Colosseum.

So *inter duas metas* might mean Peter met his end on the *spina* or central ridge of the Circus of Caius and Nero, the first-century racetrack at the foot of the Vatican and Janiculum hills. Or the two *metae* may have been further apart. By the time of the Renaissance there was a strong belief that they were the *meta Romuli* and the *meta Remi*, two ancient funerary monuments, one located near the Castel Sant'Angelo (and stripped of its marble to decorate St Peter's in the seventh century), the other either nearby or some way to the south (so sometimes conflated with the best-known Roman tomb in the city, the tall pyramid of Caius Cestius by the Porta San Sebastiano, towards San Paolo fuori le Mura – which would fit with the conflation of Peter/Paul and Romulus/Remus).

Confusingly, another source says Peter was martyred in the Naumachia – a public pool for staging sea battles – 'near Nero's obelisk on the mountain'. This could be to the north-west of the Circus of Gaius and Nero, where the Naumachia is usually put by sixteenth-century antiquarians, or could be said to corroborate one of the interpretations of *inter duas metas* above, the 'mountain' being taken to refer to the Janiculum, south of the Vatican. The sources clearly want to make some connection with Nero, a demonic figure to the early Christians. Certainly it is corroborated by non-Christian historians – admittedly, ones enjoying the patronage of later imperial dynasties – that the emperor launched a pogrom against Christians after blaming them for the devastating fire of 64 CE. But Peter's execution is often said to have taken place in 67, by which time you'd think things would have cooled off a little. Recent scholarship has anyway tended to rehabilitate Nero – and it has even been intimated that the Christians might have had a hand in the fire after all.

Wherever and whenever the deed took place, the sources are agreed that Peter chose to be crucified upside down, thereby avoiding the sin of pride (to a Christian, even if the crucifix would not become a religious emblem for some time, the cross was inevitably associated with Christ, and Peter must not have wanted to imitate his leader too closely). It may also be that this notoriously agonising death (the word excruciating comes from *crux*, cross) could be accelerated, or at least eased, by letting the victim's blood flow down into the brain. It is often said that Peter's inverted crucifixion is the reason the altar of St Peter's stands at the western rather than the eastern end, though other Constantinian churches happily face north, south or south-west (and the anthropomorphism which would dominate debates about the rebuilding of the church in the sixteenth and seventeenth centuries only begins to surface in architectural theory during the Middle Ages).

Old St Peter's was put up not where Peter was supposed to have been killed, but where he was thought to lie buried – a subject on which the sources are in greater, if not complete, agreement. As of the second century CE, a tomb-lined street, today tentatively labelled the Via Cornelia, ran parallel with the north side of the Circus of Nero. By the fourth century, one of the memorials there had acquired the reputation of containing the apostle's remains; it was directly over this that the apse of Constantine's basilica stood. Over sixteen centuries almost no archaeological exploration took place beneath St Peter's, but the location of the tomb soon became axiomatic, and was the weightiest determining factor in the sixteenth- and seventeenth-century debates about expanding or rebuilding the church.

When you enter the nave of St Peter's today, you are standing just beyond the original extent of Constantine's basilica (Fig. 2). The western side of a rectangular portico or narthex, pretty old but perhaps not quite contemporaneous with the rest of the basilica, stood about level with the doors into the new church. I mentioned in the last chapter that the new church borrows some of the foundations of the old, as well as leaning on the typically massive Roman substructure which is all that remains of the Circus next door. It also contains a few physical survivals from its Constantinian predecessor, here and there. But little sense of this vast and elaborate antiquity strikes the visitor to the church today. You feel as if you are in a standard-issue Baroque church, the sort of interior built, for example, by the Jesuits all over the Catholic world from Antwerp to Ouro Preto to Goa – but that you have been somehow shrunk to the size of an ant. The cherubs holding up the holy-water stoups on either side of the nave are six feet tall. The saints and popes along the nave walls are well over life-size. The vaulted ceiling seems an astronomical distance away.

This giganticism is a recurring theme as one moves round St Peter's. It is encouraged by the church's administrators, the *Fabbrica*, which has had inset into the floor of the nave a series of little brass markers showing how miserably *small* some of the most famous religious buildings of the world are by comparison. Hagia Sophia, St Paul's in London, St Patrick's in New York: all chewed and swallowed up by St Peter's one by one, their names rendered incongruously into

Latin – Londiniensis, Neo Eboracen[sis] – as if in defiance of the Second Vatican Council.

Size, of course, isn't everything. But it is not just its enormity which proclaims this to be an exceptional building. The decorative surface which covers the basilica's massive structural core was mostly designed in the seventeenth century (much of it by the industrious Bernini), but small refinements have continued ever since. There is still a team of expert mosaicists in the Vatican. Marble facings were still being applied to Michelangelo's and Maderno's original travertine pilasters in the early twentieth century. One of the marble saints in the niches which line the walls of the nave was carved in 1954. The maintenance corps which looks after the basilica, the so-called 'Sampietrini', make it their business to keep everything scrupulously clean – there is none of that pleasing wine-cellar smell which makes churchgoing in hot countries such a pleasure. Signs of oldness, of tarnish or erosion, are apparently prohibited, as though the building's antiquity were a shameful secret rather than the key to its significance and power. But in fact what the papal authorities are trying to guarantee is that the power and significance of St Peter's continues to shine forth undimmed. This is not some musty little catacomb, stripped of its ornament by the Landsknechts in 1527 or the restorers in 1929, they say; this is the Pope's own church.

It is another small irony, then, that the first small scrap of the old basilica which we encounter in the nave of the new one is a neglected but eloquent marker of the most remarkable and, to us, curious aspect of papal history, the so-called *temporale*, the earthly, princely powers of the Popes. A few paces into the church, along the central axis, camouflaged from casual attention by the rich pattern of inlaid stones surrounding it, is a disc of porphyry, a hard, granitic rock mostly quarried in Egypt (Fig. 3). The base colour is a solemn, sanguinary blend of red, purple and brown, flecked with little quartz deposits like the grain and fat suspended in a slice of black pudding. Cracks and splinters have felt their way across the surface, for all its toughness. This is called the *rota*, or wheel; it played a crucial part in the workings of the old church, and retains a whisper of symbolic potency in the new one.

As well as legitimising Christianity, Constantine's other great claim to fame was to split the Roman Empire in two. From the early fourth century CE, Byzantium in Turkey, which Constantine named Constantinople after himself and which is now the Turkish capital Istanbul, was a capital city on an equal footing with Rome. Conveniently situated between the Mediterranean, the Black Sea and the rich Hellenistic cities of Arabia, Byzantium soon became a safer and more prosperous place than Rome itself, marooned halfway down a peninsula, served by long and risky trade routes across Western Europe. Byzantine Rome was spared the devastating attacks which brought down the Western empire in the fifth century CE. It endured for some eleven and a half centuries before the Ottoman Turks captured Constantinople in 1453 (Rome itself had lasted approximately as long, from its legendary foundation in 753 BCE to its sacking by the Goths in 410 CE).

During the first few centuries of free Christian worship, the only great power in the Mediterranean was Byzantium. The Eastern empire quickly lost most of the characteristics it had brought with it from the West. The classical style in art

3. The *rota* set in the nave floor. Its surface reveals cracks and irregularities
which are signs of oldness, scarcely visible elsewhere in St Peter's. The
curlicues at the corners are by Bernini, mid-seventeenth century.

mutated into something more distilled and less representational ('primitive' and 'decadent' used to be the words people used: then, later, 'mysterious' and 'spiritual'). New building types were devised – or rather, old forms were adapted to new uses. The fatal dependence of Western Rome on expensive military strength and a – let's not mince words – proto-fascistic submission of the individual to the State gave way to a looser and more pragmatic system where calling yourself a Roman (which the Byzantines curiously did, though they did so in Greek) could mean more or less what you wanted it to mean.

Byzantium was also officially, if not quite exclusively, Christian. The religion had become the State faith at the end of the fourth century, and most of the ancient religious foundations now lay within the Byzantine empire – Jerusalem, Antioch and, after a short hiatus, Rome itself. Until around 800 CE (there are good reasons for being vague about the date, as well as one very good reason for being specific about it), the city of Rome was of by no means paramount importance in the Christian world. After the collapse of the Western empire's infrastructure in the fifth century, Italy was ruled by Germanic tribes, then recaptured if only partly retained by Byzantium. As of the seventh century, Rome was part of a Byzantine enclave called the exarchate, which ran across central Italy to Ravenna; the land to the north was mostly ruled by Lombards, and that to the south by various parties. The Pope was therefore just another patriarch (and if Peter had personally founded the church at Rome, he had done the same at Antioch and Jerusalem, and the patriarchs in those cities could claim the apostolic succession too, as could other patriarchs from other apostles). Texts from the period do claim some sort of pre-eminence for Rome, it is true, but it is unlikely that the leaders of what would later become known as the Orthodox Church paid such claims much mind. And the Emperor's viceroy, the exarch, certainly didn't feel bound by the wishes of the Pope in any significant way.

During the eighth century, things began to change. The Lombards seized central Italy, and killed the exarch. Pepin the Younger – a less kindly epithet is Pepin the Short – a Frankish king from the Rhineland, drove them back and more or less united the Italian peninsula under Frankish rule. A crucial part of his strategy was to align himself with the cause of Christianity, and the person of the Pope. He had already had himself and his son Charles anointed by Pope Stephen III at St Denis, just north of Paris; now he rewarded the Popes for their endorsement by confirming them as rulers of a strip of Italy roughly corresponding to the exarchate. At the end of the auspicious year 800 CE, Charles, known later as Charles the Great or Charlemagne, was crowned Roman Emperor – the better-known phrase is Holy Roman Emperor – by Pope Leo III in St Peter's. We are not sure what form the ceremony took, though the sources claim it was a modest and unshowy ritual, almost an afterthought, tacked on to the end of a Nativity Mass. Nor do we quite know whose idea it was. But the Pope had certainly set out to woo Charles, getting a mosaic made in the Lateran palace which showed himself taking a set of keys, and Charles a military standard, from St Peter. The choice of venue for the first Western imperial coronation could hardly have been more unambiguous in its significance. The Prince of the Apostles – or his designated successor, at least – and the Prince of the West were now officially in cahoots. The temporal and the spiritual wings of this peculiar regime would henceforward beat as one.

Whether this new Western, Latinised empire was to be a mere extension of Byzantium or a rival to it is hard to assess. Certainly Byzantium was weak at the time: riven by the Iconoclastic debate, browbeaten by the Muslim caliphs, ruled – to widespread horror – by a woman, the Empress Irene. But Charlemagne did not take ship for the East as soon as the imperial diadem was on his brow; he went home to Aachen. Most of his campaigning was done in the West, even if he fought the Muslims – unsuccessfully – in Spain. His assumed title was not precisely the Latin equivalent of that taken by the Byzantine emperor, *Basileus tōn Rōmaiōn* or King of the Romans ('basilica' is, of course, cognate with the Greek word *basileus*), but rather a conscious reassertion of Western models (he even went by the nickname 'Augustus' at court). His intention to restore a decayed Western Roman empire after three and a half centuries, and to do so under the wing of a reinvigorated Western Church, was unmistakable. Indeed, he may well have grasped that religion was the only thing which could unite a territory as disparate as Europe had become. Certainly he is often credited with the discovery or invention of a dream-kingdom known as 'Christendom', a debatable land over which the Western Church would henceforward take a keen, proprietorial interest.

At every stage (and it lasted in one form or other until the early nineteenth century), the Holy Roman Empire was a decentralised and in many ways a flimsy thing. But at almost every stage – except when the Bohemian Estates put a Protestant up for the job, with catastrophic results, in 1618 – the holiness of the Holy Roman Empire was a crucial part of its armour. Rebellious princes could be excommunicated by the Pope. Once excommunicated, they could no longer enforce feudal oaths of loyalty. Plotting or fighting against them would not be treason. After Leo endorsed Charlemagne, the Popes would enjoy a casting vote in the affairs of Europe for centuries.

If this new power were not enough, the Popes now also enjoyed something they had never had before: a dominion of their own. Whether they owed some sort of suzerainty to the Western Emperor, or any vestigial dues to the Eastern Emperor, was not resolved (and would become the basis for some bitter conflicts during the Middle Ages). But Pepin's grant of land to them, confirmed by Charlemagne, made them princes.

This leads us to a controversial document which seems to have been written some time before 800, but which claimed to be much older. It declared that Pope Sylvester I had baptised Constantine and cured him of leprosy, and that in his gratitude the Emperor had made a donation of land rather more extensive than that now on offer from the Frankish kings: Rome, Naples and Sicily, northern Italy, Spain, Gaul, Germany and Britain. Not a bad day's work for Sylvester. But in fact, Constantine was almost certainly baptised, if at all, on his deathbed by Eusebius in Palestine; and there's no evidence that he ever had leprosy. The authorship of the so-called Donation of Constantine remains obscure. It was probably meant to throw some weight behind Pepin and Charles's policy in the eighth and early ninth centuries – the territory Pepin gave to the Popes was, after all, pretty modest compared to the inflated precedent allegedly set by Constantine – and citing an antique example of a mighty ruler marching in step with the Pope was an expedient move for the Franks. Having outlived its usefulness, it was soon jettisoned. Otto

III denounced it to the French Pope Sylvester II at the turn of the eleventh century. The Popes themselves continued to cite the Donation occasionally – and more in hope than expectation – until the Vatican admitted it was phoney during the Renaissance (a scholar named Lorenzo Valla pronounced it a forgery in around 1440, on the basis of a number of anachronisms and stock phrases – not to mention the fact that portions of it appeared to have been lifted wholesale from the Bible). Its last serious outing is probably on the walls of the Stanza di Costantino in the Vatican palace (1517–24), where Raphael and his team of assistants recorded a series of historical or quasi-historical events including the Donation of Constantine (nearby in the Stanza dell'Incendio is a fresco of the coronation of Charlemagne, set, in a typical anachronism, not in old St Peter's, but an interior not unlike contemporary designs for the new basilica).

Charlemagne's coronation in St Peter's is said to have been an ad hoc affair – indeed, he is said by his biographer Einhard to have been unwilling to take the crown at all. Perhaps this shows us that even if he had not read Plutarch on Caesar, he had absorbed at least some lessons about the arts of government from Roman history. His coronation was in one sense more akin to an ordination, the yoking of a military and political leader to a religious cause. Some historians have even claimed that it was the Pope who stage-managed the whole business, and that Charlemagne was genuinely taken by surprise to find himself suddenly being laden with regalia. Others point the finger at Alcuin, a courtier of Charlemagne's, though this would make the spontaneity of the event still harder to credit.

Despite Charlemagne's primary interest in the Western

empire, the idea of a religious leader crowning a secular ruler in a pompous ritual was essentially a Byzantine import. The people of Europe were at this stage perhaps less attuned to the majesty of kingship than at other periods (the great popular assemblies of the Vikings are roughly contemporary with the rise of the Franks, for example). And the Popes, in their new role as princes and kingmakers, needed something more concrete than the piety, simplicity and unworldliness of their forefathers. The fragrant and mysterious Eastern empire, therefore, soon became a convenient wellspring of iconography and ritual for the new potentates of the West.

It was really between 800 and 1200 CE that the papacy began to exist in the form that we recognise it today. Many familiar details of dress – the tall tiara, girt round after a time with three crowns; the long jewelled robes of purple and white – can be traced back to Eastern sources. Popes also began to borrow elements of Byzantine court ritual. The *rota* which persists in the nave of New St Peter's is one of four which were set in the floor of the old basilica. Discs were fairly common in antique stone floors, as they could easily be sliced like salami from redundant or too-tall columns. They also formed important decorative nuclei in the Byzantine-derived inlay technique often called Cosmati or Cosmatesque, after a Roman family which allegedly perfected the craft in the early Middle Ages. This was a blending of antique Roman *opus sectile* or 'cut-up work', the distribution of different coloured marble slabs to form a geometrical pattern on a floor or wall, with Byzantine mosaic, a more intricate arrangement of gilded or coloured glass. It is the purple stone of which the *rotae* were made that signals something rare and precious. In fact, porphyry signified imperial status in the Roman and

Byzantine worlds, either because the stone was associated with Pharaonic projects in Egypt, or possibly because its colour approximated to that of a costly and status-giving dye, murex or Tyrian purple. The *rotae* in St Peter's were markers of wealth and luxury – like so many other materials used there, then and since – but also of earthly authority. They imitated similar porphyry wheels in the imperial palace in Constantinople; these were used to orchestrate the proverbially intricate court rituals which took place there. Courtiers or visitors used the *rotae* as flags indicating where to stop or prostrate themselves. A large *rota* surrounded by smaller discs survives in Hagia Sophia, the imperial church, marking the coronation spot of the Byzantine emperor. The *rotae* in Old St Peter's were by no means the Popes' only borrowing from the Eastern court – the shrine of the Apostle was at some stage allegedly garnished with porphyry columns, and the purple stone was widely deployed at St John Lateran – but it is striking that they came to be used in the coronation rituals of the Western Emperors, which usually took place in St Peter's, and which soon evolved from Charlemagne's no-nonsense prototype into overblown extravaganzas lasting several days.

Various ceremonials survive recording one or other of these events. What they have in common is the deference which the would-be Emperor is made to show the Pope. After Charlemagne, the Western Church found itself imitating and indeed surpassing its Eastern counterpart's intimate relationship with imperial power. Indeed, the Popes used *rotae* as markers of princely rather than mere priestly status. During imperial coronations, the purple discs were used for prayers, prostrations and oaths. They came in useful at other times, too; after the Peace of Venice in 1177 the errant Emperor Frederick Barbarossa performed the Byzantine ritual of *proskynesis*, a prostration or kowtow, to Pope Alexander III, on a *rota* in the Byzantine church of St Mark.

The last Emperor to be crowned at St Peter's was Frederick III, in 1452. In 1530, when the Vatican basilica was a building site, a fake *rota* was painted on to the floor of St Petronius's church in the papal enclave of Bologna for the coronation of Charles V, an Emperor whose conduct towards the papacy could hardly be called deferential (one good reason why Rome was seen as an inappropriate venue for the coronation was the fact that it had been sacked by imperial troops just three years before). That they bothered to do this illustrates the power of the *rota* to suggest sacred, ancient allegiances and invoke half-understood traditions; but should also remind us that ritual and realism are by no means mutually exclusive.

Like his predecessors, Charles used religion as an instrument of empire: but unlike at least some of them, he had no need to act as though empire was simultaneously an instrument of religion. His unchallenged domination of Catholic Europe, the loss of the continent's northern and western reaches to Protestantism and then the holocaust of the Thirty Years' War would conspire to render the Pope's role as guarantor of the Emperor increasingly irrelevant. From the mid-seventeenth century, European politics gradually settled into a recognisable version of the early-modern 'Great Game' in which consolidated power blocs – France, Spain, the Habsburg Empire (the Emperor's notional elected status having gone by the board long since), then later England, Prussia and Russia – made and broke alliances among themselves for essentially pragmatic reasons, with religion often only a notional factor. The Popes held on to some of their land – though they lost plenty to the Habsburgs in the sixteenth century. But their temporal power lessened inexorably from the time of Julius II in the early sixteenth century until the fall of Rome to the forces of Italian unification on 20 September 1870.

The one surviving *rota* in St Peter's, salvaged from the old church and installed in the new one during the seventeenth century (the floor was designed by Maderno but modified by Bernini), thus has a nostalgic flavour about it. It may well have been installed in the hope that more imperial coronations might take place in the rebuilt basilica; but its essential role is decorative. The more diligent tour guides still stop to point it out, but the information they give is inconsistent (it is probably not true that Charlemagne himself ever stood, sat or knelt on any of the *Rotae* in old St Peter's, even if they may well have been installed in the basilica floor by then). As for the other three discs – well, they could be anywhere. In the early seventeenth century bits of masonry from Old St Peter's were farmed out to other Roman churches like unwanted heirlooms. What looks rather like one is set into the floor of the Grottoes, the crypt of New St Peter's, roughly beneath the survival in the nave.

The decay of a political symbol into a picturesque one can be a sad sight. At least the *rota* isn't inconsistent with the decor of the church. But I was reminded of it in May 2005, while watching the newly-enthroned Benedict XVI sitting somewhere in the vastness of St Peter's on a little wooden dais around twenty centimetres high. A long line of world leaders stood waiting to shake or kiss the pontiff's hand. The event's domestic importance was evident from its being televised in its entirety on Italy's main state channel RAI 1; other countries were doubtless content to extract a couple of minutes' footage of their own leaders for a slot on the evening news. As courteous as the whole ritual was, it simply wasn't like the old days. A couple of wellwishers went beyond the standard procedure and attempted a bashful hug. But nobody came even close to the *proskynesis*.

3

....

REBIRTH

Men must be changed by religion, not religion by men.

Giles of Viterbo

If the great nave of St Peter's does not today much resemble a conventional Roman basilica or its Early Christian successors, its ancestry nevertheless seems pretty clear. Clambering back to our feet on the *rota*, we see a high, vaulted space which opens outwards and upwards ahead of us into two transepts and a central dome, with a short choir or chancel just visible behind the high altar and its elaborate bronze canopy. In other words, a Latin-cross church of a type common in the Middle Ages, refined in the Renaissance and rolled out – as I've suggested above – on an industrial scale by the resurgent Catholic Church throughout the seventeenth and early eighteenth centuries. Yet the demolition of Old St Peter's, and the construction of a new church on the site, was a hugely drawn-out business (proverbially so – *la fabbrica di San Pietro* is used by the Italians as a simile for anything unendurably slow or long-winded). Bernini's interior muffles and blurs our sense of the different phases of construction, and the different architectural and liturgical fashions which have been in force at different times during the process.

The story of the destruction of the old church, and the

building of the new one, is long and sometimes unedifying. For more than half a century what was sought was not the building of a new church, but the adaptation of the old one. Even when the drastic decision was taken to pull down some of Old St Peter's, it is unclear whether, or for how long, the surviving part was meant to remain standing. Arguments about conservation, and reverence for the dead, and ecclesiastical form, were widespread, both within the Vatican and, increasingly, far beyond its walls. The transformation of old into new was stalled and compromised at almost every turn by favouritism, untimely death, lack of money, political instability and, to an unguessable but significant degree, the religious revolution which seized Europe in the sixteenth century. New St Peter's was not formally inaugurated until 1626, 1,300 years after the supposed completion of Constantine's original church, and around 180 years after work had begun on remodelling it.

The Pope responsible for this beginning (the beginning of the end for the old church, if not quite yet a beginning for the new one) was Tommaso Parentucello or Parentucelli, enthroned in 1447 as Pope Nicholas V. Nicholas had sure political instincts, but fragile luck. He sought to consolidate the prestige of the papacy after a century and a half of schism and exile, and to wrestle control of Rome back from a scrum of squabbling barons. A decade of ecumenical initiatives by Nicholas and his predecessors started to bear fruit when the Orthodox Church declared itself reunited with the Catholic in 1452 – but Constantinople fell to the Turks a year later. Nicholas declared a Jubilee in 1450, but some 200 pilgrims got to see Paradise a little sooner than they had expected when they were crushed to death on the Ponte Sant'Angelo.

4. Foundation medal of St Peter's, 1506, by Caradosso. Details aren't easy to make out, but the similarity of Bramante's projected dome to the Pantheon is clear, as is the way the whole building has something of the appearance of a walled citadel with towers at the corners.

His major achievement was to make the first serious start on the rebuilding of Rome after the 'Babylonian Captivity' – the Popes' abandonment of Rome for Avignon between 1305 and 1378, and the so-called Great Schism which lasted another forty years, during which time both Rome and Avignon continued to field candidates for the papacy until Martin V, a Roman from the powerful Colonna family, restored unified rule in 1418. Thirty years later, Nicholas was intent on consolidating Rome as the only natural base for papal government. Restoration work was done on the Campidoglio, in St John Lateran and, especially, the Vatican. The papal palace was expanded and decorated. The condition of Old St Peter's was a particular cause for lamentation. There were cracks in the walls and floor, and one chronicler even says wild wolves had colonised the interior (a clever trope, this, on the she-wolf who had suckled Romulus and Remus in Rome's first infancy). The nave of the church was stabilised – what we would call 'underpinning'. More radically, an extension was planned, though not completed and perhaps only scarcely begun. According to scholarly guesses, the extension would have been inconspicuous from the eastern end, the river and the city; it might also have rendered unnecessary the later, wholesale rebuilding of the basilica. But it would have transformed the worshipper's experience of the building's interior space, and given St Peter's a more striking presence on the Roman skyline. The apse was to be extended westwards to make a choir. The transepts were to be made bigger, and higher. There may have been a vault planned to replace the nave's ageing timber roof. Most dramatically, a dome was projected for the central crossing area, rising over the apostolic shrine at the church's core.

It's not clear how far the project went during Nicholas's lifetime. His chronicler, one Gianozzo Manetti, wrote about ideas which clearly never left the drawing board as though they had been brought to full fruition. He is also a little vague on names, places, dimensions and so on. But it's probable that by Nicholas's death in 1455, designs for the remodelling of St Peter's had been put into partial effect. As to who came up with those designs – again, Manetti wasn't being paid to puff up the reputation of some artisan. But it seems likely that a crucial figure was Leon Battista Alberti, a schoolfriend of Nicholas, a fellow-Florentine (we shall repeatedly see how regional favouritism has coloured the history of St Peter's) and one of the most influential intellectuals of the Italian Renaissance. Alberti presented Nicholas with a manuscript copy of his treatise *De Re Aedificatoria*, concerning the matter of building, in 1452; not just the usual glad-handing, but also a gesture of intimacy from one fellow-traveller to another.

Not a single stone put in place at St Peter's during this curious transitional phase between 'Old' and 'New' can confidently be attributed to Alberti. A loggia stuck rather awkwardly on the western façade of the Early Christian narthex or courtyard in front of Constantine's church, but demolished to make way for the new nave and façade in the early seventeenth century, was long said to be by him (it resembled a slice of the Colosseum's outer wall, peeled off and laid flat) – but it's more recently been given to Francesco del Borgo, the architect of Pius II (1458–64). Christof Thoenes points out that there's a passage in *De Re Aedificatoria* which attacks hasty and piecemeal alterations to existing buildings, and infers from this that Alberti can't have been involved in rebuilding St Peter's, much of which would have survived

Nicholas's building programme unaltered. But there were special reasons for preserving as much as could be preserved of a building as venerable and important as this. Its relationship with Constantine was a reminder of the intimacy Popes continued to expect, though increasingly not to receive, from Emperors; its relationship with Peter himself, it has been argued, went one better, constituting a gentle reminder that the Popes had been around for two and a half centuries before Constantine. Lastly, it was packed with tombs and relics which it would be laborious, not to mention sacrilegious, to displace. Alberti anyway remodelled existing buildings elsewhere, like the famous Tempio Malatestiana at Rimini. In any case, the first modifications to the basilica, such as they were, were probably done by Bernardo Rossellino, whom some accounts treat as little more than an amanuensis of Alberti's – and maybe continued later in the century by another Florentine, Giuliano da Sangallo. If Alberti was involved in Nicholas's project it was probably more as an *eminence grise* than a practical, hands-on architect. This is how he seems to have worked on earlier projects in Florence and Rimini, at any rate.

Manetti's chronicle sets the tone for future works on St Peter's. A chivalric, medieval voice, celebrating knightly pursuits and the manifold glories of Nature, gives way to something new: the classicising, allegorical language of the Renaissance, where everything might be a symbol for something else. Nicholas was the new Peter, the Vicar of Christ (something of which the Roman nobility and the quarrelling factions of the Church still needed reminding after the Schism); but he was also the new Augustus, who had found a Rome of brick and left one of marble, and the new

Constantine, the princely churchbuilder. Most tellingly, he was a reborn Solomon, the builder of the Temple, who had re-established the Jewish nation after the Babylonian captivity – the duration of which, seventy-odd years, approximated conveniently to the Popes' sojourn at Avignon. And if Nicholas was Solomon, then Rome was Jerusalem, and St Peter's was the Temple – an analogy which would hold fast well into the eighteenth century.

What Nicholas's architects certainly did begin to build was an elongated apse or tribune, beyond the old semicircular apse to the west of Constantine's basilica. Foundations were dug, and walls begun. Traces have since been found of two walls to the west of the fourth-century transepts; these would if completed have widened the central part of the church. From Manetti it seems that the central space of the church was to be extended upwards with a dome, a fashionable architectural innovation little seen in Europe since antiquity, but recently and triumphantly applied to the cathedral of Santa Maria del Fiore in Florence, the city where Nicholas and Alberti had been schoolmates. This had itself been a pretty drawn-out project, mooted by Arnolfo di Cambio in the early fourteenth century, then finally devised and executed to the designs of Filippo Brunelleschi in the fifteenth. It was famous across Europe as a landmark and a technological feat, and the prestige it conferred upon the city of Florence could hardly be lost on an ambitious builder in Rome, especially one of Florentine stock.

The Nicholas V plan, in so far as it can be reconstructed, was not one of those sparse, abstract, geometrical designs one associates with the early Italian Renaissance. It was, in modern architectural parlance, 'contextual' – a reticent intervention in a venerated building. The fabric was to be extended in just two directions – upwards, and westwards. The tombs and altars of the Constantinian basilica – and, in particular, Peter's shrine in the apse – were not to be disturbed. Other enhancements were to include a spacious, rectangular piazza in front of the basilica, and various architectural and decorative schemes in the Vatican palace, a few of which, like the exquisite little private chapel frescoed by Fra Angelico (another Florentine), still survive. But Nicholas's grander plans for St Peter's were clearly not especially far advanced by the time of his death – and, since the papacy is not a hereditary office, few allies of his would be in any position to bolster his memory in the court of his successor. It would be another fifty years before the transformation of St Peter's began in earnest.

By that time, the turn of the sixteenth century, Alberti's ideas, and those of other Renaissance intellectuals working in architecture and the visual arts, had gained much wider acceptance than in the 1450s. Florentine patrons, in particular the ruling Medici clan, had devised a new template for the cultivated nabob or princeling, which was being widely exported around Italy. Florentine artistic fashions unsurprisingly spread in its wake. Books celebrating the new systematic thought, and the new weight attached to classical models, which we associate with the period, were being written (and even printed). By the end of the fifteenth century talented artists and designers from Florence, Urbino, Lombardy, Venice and Dalmatia were converging on Rome. Some were in urgent need of a change of scenery, like Leonardo da Vinci and Donato Bramante, on the run from the fallen Sforza court in Milan. All were lured by the energetic patronage being exercised by Nicholas's successors, particularly the two

Ligurian Popes, uncle and nephew, Sixtus IV and Julius II. Sixtus had built a private papal chapel in the Vatican, famous now as the Sistine Chapel, bleak and fortress-like from outside, decorated within by graceful, narratively elaborate frescoes from the hands of Botticelli, Perugino and others in the late 1470s and 80s. Between 1508 and 1512, Julius had the chapel's ceiling replaced by Michelangelo's extraordinary cycle in which scenes from the book of Genesis are framed by a full supporting cast of prophets, sibyls, cherubs, *ignudi* (well-built young men in advanced states of undress who are generally, and rather coyly, said to represent Sacred Love) and ancestors of Christ. In 1509 he installed Raphael at the head of a gifted squadron of painters who had just begun to decorate a series of vaulted rooms, the *stanze*, in the Vatican. Most pertinently to our business here, he also initiated the radical transformation of St Peter's. A commemorative medal showing Julius on one side, and a design for an entirely new church on the other, was issued in 1506 (Fig. 4).

The background to this decision is unclear. The debates about whether to demolish Old St Peter's, wholly or in part, and what form the rebuilt church should take, do not come down to us in detail, but are hinted at by historians and chroniclers of the period and can be inferred from a large collection of architectural drawings in the Uffizi (the authorship and dating of which has been hotly disputed by architectural historians). Julius has come in for a good deal of criticism for his warmongering and greed, but also for having demolished around half of Old St Peter's (and probably having wanted the other half pulled down too). The conventional explanation for this is that he intended to put his tomb in pride of place in the new church, maybe displacing even Peter's tomb into the bargain. In fact there's no evidence that he did so. He commissioned Michelangelo to design his tomb a year before the new church was begun, at which time he may simply have intended the monument to stand in a completed tribune or choir, the western extension initiated by Nicholas V half a century before: that is, tucked behind the apostolic shrine. In the event Julius's tomb was never finished – Michelangelo called it the tragedy of his life – though a drastically scaled-down version was put in another St Peter's, the Della Rovere church of San Pietro in Vincoli.

So it may be a little harsh on Julius to accuse him of vainglory, even if his tomb would have been quite a pile if it had been finished according to Michelangelo's first designs. Popes, as we have seen, don't get to put their children on Peter's throne after them; building is about the only way they can seek to be remembered at all. The 1506 plan for St Peter's is better understood as an attempt to carry on with the project initiated by Nicholas: to consolidate the revived fortunes of Rome, to make the basilica more amenable to pilgrims, and, naturally, to maximise papal prestige by giving the first Pope a shrine worthy of what was explicitly understood to be a new and luminous age. Renewal of St Peter's, too, would mean a new start for the church; even before the Reformation, calls for reform were starting to be heard.

The architect eventually chosen for the job, Donato Bramante, was originally from Urbino but had made a name for himself in Milan. His architecture there took local traditions – terracotta ornament, a certain kind of double-arched window still sometimes called a Lombard window – and tempered them with the austere classicism of the Florentine tradition, and, evidently, some sort of direct intellectual engagement with the classical sources which lay behind that. In Rome his first-hand appreciation of ancient tombs, arches and temples led him to an architecture much closer to the antique than had hitherto been practised anywhere in Italy. He also engaged with the new theories of the Renaissance, in particular with Alberti's championship of centrally planned churches in *De Re Aedificatoria*: 'Let us make our temples round,' Alberti had written, explaining that the circle was the most perfect of geometrical figures, expressive of both oneness and infinity, and so (implicitly) of the perfection of God's creation.

In 1502 – or so – Bramante designed the so-called Tempietto, or little temple (Fig. 5) in a little cloister next to the church of San Pietro in Montorio. The name comes from *in monte aurea*, 'on the golden hill' – the ancient name for the Janiculum, and a contender for the site of Peter's martyrdom (see Chapter 2). Bramante's church must thus be seen as a sort of shrine to Peter; but it was also a display of architectural virtuosity and Roman cultural pre-eminence, unveiled to great fanfares during a state visit by Ferdinand and Isabella of Spain. British visitors who climb up to see the church will notice that it looks like a tiny version of the dome of St Paul's in London. Its influence has been extraordinarily widespread for such a small building. It is customary to describe it as a dry-run for the new St Peter's, though how building a very small dome would have helped prepare Bramante to build a very large one (not to mention how inspecting a small one would have confirmed to the papal authorities that they fancied the idea of a large one) is unclear. But the Tempietto anticipates Bramante's design for the big church in two respects: its determined classicism, and its formal and geometrical purity.

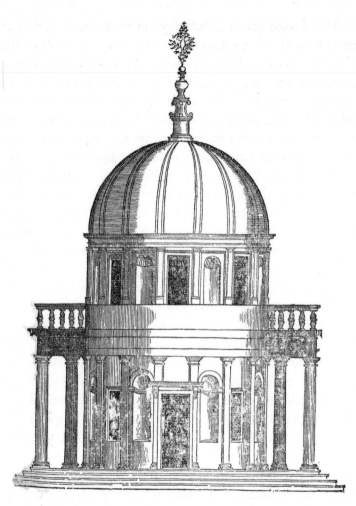

5. Bramante's Tempietto, woodcut, turn of the sixteenth century, from a
seventeenth-century edition of Sebastiano Serlio's architectural treatise.
The little building is made up of elementary geometrical forms, and shows
a rigorous understanding of classical architecture and ornament. It was
disproportionately influential on St Peter's, as on many other buildings since,
notably St Paul's Cathedral in London.

The Tempietto is a little cylinder of space with just enough room for an altar and about half a dozen people. There is a crypt underneath which is even smaller. A ring of columns runs round the central pepperpot shape, broadening and softening it. The whole structure sits on three circular steps. The architecture is entirely classical, without the Romanesque and Byzantine elements you see in Florentine fifteenth-century buildings, or even the odd vernacular flourish which enlivens Bramante's earlier work in Milan. If the result is beautiful − and many people would unhesitatingly describe the Tempietto as the most beautiful building in the world − its beauty is severe, something to do with simple, elegant proportions and the exact use of a limited vocabulary of forms.

The Tempietto is very like a Roman temple (note that it has never been called a *chiesetta* or little church) − and yet very unlike one too. The principles of classical architecture have been digested and applied to a new building: one which may bear a passing resemblance to round temples or tombs from Tivoli, Pompeii, Delphi or wherever, but is nevertheless an unmistakable product of its own time. The reliefs running round the frieze take the sacrificial imagery you might expect to see on a Roman temple − bowls, skulls, knives and so on − and Christianise it, depicting tools and emblems associated with the passion of Christ. The floor is Cosmati work, that Byzantine technique reappropriated by early-medieval Rome (and still widely practised during the Roman Renaissance). The altar is not outside, where it would be in a pagan temple, but inside, where the symbolic sacrifice of Mass is to be celebrated by a small group of initiates.

Bramante's Tempietto is an updating of an early Christian

prototype, the martyrium or shrine. It is as much a tomb as a church (or rather a cenotaph or empty tomb, since the remains of St Peter were believed to lie in the Vatican to the north). If the early Christian basilica was essentially a pragmatic form, capable of accommodating large congregations, processing pilgrims, burying many dead, then the martyrium was a symbolic and abstract space. Bramante's masterstroke (and he had already done something similar in his remodelling of the sixth-century martyrium of San Satiro in Milan) was to see that the abstraction and symbolism required by this Christian building type could best be emphasised in the solemn, lucid and orderly architecture of pagan Rome. The Tempietto was conceived as an ideal building, assimilating and synthesising different models and traditions, just as a Raphael madonna of the early sixteenth century might be said to assimilate and synthesise the best bits of several real women to create an ideal one. Its smallness and uselessness contributed to this sense of idealism. Bramante's design for New St Peter's called for something immeasurably more complex in structure, form and function; but something of the purity of its minuscule predecessor can still be seen in it.

It has also been said of Bramante's St Peter's that he was trying to combine two of the most praised antique buildings in Rome: that he wanted 'to put the Pantheon on top of the Temple of Peace'. There is something unwieldy and faintly distasteful about the idea, somehow, like an indigestible Roman delicacy made from several animals stuffed inside one another. One pictures the result of such a union as better suited to the Strip in Las Vegas than the Eternal City. But the two temples in question didn't lack admirers during the Roman Renaissance. The Pantheon (Fig. 6) is a vast concrete dome hovering over a round hall faced in luscious coloured marbles (it has several porphyry *rotae* inset into the floor). It was first built by Marcus Agrippa, Augustus's closest ally, and rebuilt by Hadrian, by which time it was probably dedicated not to 'all the gods', the literal translation of its name, but to some aspect of the imperial cult. What was until the nineteenth century mistakenly called the Temple of Peace is nowadays known as the Basilica of Maxentius, a rectangular hall less well preserved than the Pantheon, also vaulted in concrete, towards the south-eastern end of the Forum. Both buildings attest to the technical skill of Roman builders, not to mention the formal purity of Roman architecture at its best. If any monuments were worthy of imitation in this prestigious project, these were. But if the rebuilders of St Peter's wanted to compete with the Pantheon on the level of sheer size, they failed; the dome of the new basilica would be a metre or so less in diameter than its Roman predecessor.

The significance of the Pantheon and the Basilica of Maxentius could be recognised on many levels. The former had been given to the Pope by the Byzantine Emperor in the seventh century – Caesar once again dutifully rendering unto God's appointed agent that which was God's – and dedicated to the Christian martyrs. The cavernous roundness of the interior, its lack of any obvious cardinal orientation or particular emphasis on any one spot, was ingeniously rebranded by a monotheistic culture as a celebration of multiple acts of sacrifice and heroism, each one in its way representative of Christ's own sacrifice, as we have seen with Bernini's colonnade. Nineteenth-century Italy would rebrand the temple again, turning it into a shrine to the country's first kings. A few artistic heroes, including Raphael, were already buried

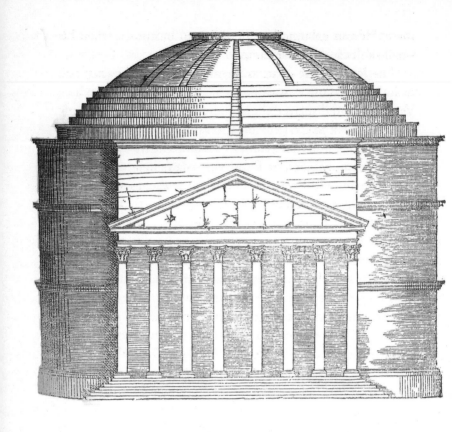

6. The Pantheon was felt, in the Renaissance and subsequently, to be a more
or less flawless example of Roman building. Images of it like this one occupy
a curious middle ground, with fine cracks attesting to the building's antiquity,
but a general sense of precision and order as well. Serlio's representation of
Bramante's projected dome for St Peter's has similar hairline flaws although
it was never built.

there. He was exhumed in the nineteenth century, when his small skull caused some disappointment.

The latter, quite apart from its stateliness, capacity and technical virtuosity, was thought to be the place where Vespasian had displayed the treasure from the sacked Temple of Jerusalem in 70 CE (the actual Temple of Peace is gone now, but stood nearby). Items from this famous hoard are depicted on the triumphal arch of Titus, Vespasian's heir and general. The Romans' virtual extinction of the Jews was an event of fundamental importance to the Christians, with their deeply ambivalent relationship towards Judaism. An apocalyptic assault on one culture cleared the way for another. For one thing, early Christianity could well be described as a reformist Jewish sect. For another, mainstream Christianity would for a long time continue to describe the Jews as the killers of Christ; here was one case in which the pagans had done them a favour, allowing themselves to serve as unwitting agents of God's wrath. Certainly the importance of Jerusalem as the site of the Crucifixion made it worth commemorating in Christian Rome (there are even echoes of Golgotha in early accounts of Peter's execution on the Janiculum).

The fact that the spoils of Jerusalem had been brought to Rome consolidated the Eternal City's status as the nerve-centre of the New Dispensation – Augustine's idealised City of God, as well as his sinful City of Man. Presumed relics of the Jewish Temple which ended up in Christian churches, like the twisted columns which framed the shrine of St Peter from soon after its inception, some of which still form part of the rebuilt basilica's fabric today, emphasised Christianity's continuity with its monotheistic predecessor, but also proclaimed its supersession of it.

This brings us back to the troublesome question of why St Peter's had to be rebuilt at all. Architectural conservationism didn't really exist at the time; Old St Peter's was dilapidated, and deeply unfashionable. Those who wanted the old church retained were chiefly exercised by the potentially sinful disregard for the tranquillity of the dead which either radical remodelling or complete renewal would necessarily entail. There was also the risk that rebuilding the basilica might just seem like a vanity project (in both the Christian and the modern senses of the word 'vanity') on the part of Julius II. Against this we should set not only the strongly classicising tastes of the period, but also its theologians' belief in renewal as a fulfilment of ancient destinies. The utopian Jewish belief in rebuilding the Temple could easily be adopted by Christians, and the notion that Rome rather than Jerusalem was the appropriate place to do so could as well be justified by Vespasian's antique precedent as by mere papal *amour propre*. Augustine was the most revered religious thinker in Rome at the turn of the sixteenth century, and his language, rich in metaphor and poised between abstract idealism and lived reality, resonated elegantly with the cultural preoccupations of the Renaissance (the very word, of course, meaning 'rebirth'). A new St Peter's would absorb the old one even as it superseded it; but it would also do the same with countless other buildings, dreamed or executed, Catholic or Orthodox, Christian or Jewish, across the wide centuries.

Bramante's plan of 1506 was rooted, in the good Renaissance fashion, in the eloquent ruins of ancient Rome and Early Christianity, both sacred sources and profane ones. If a resemblance can be spotted between his St Peter's and the octagonal fourth-century church of San Lorenzo Maggiore in Milan, then there is also a clear debt to the great bath complexes built by pre-Constantinian rulers, including the great scourge of the Christians, Diocletian. He was also at least speculatively interested in the vanished Jewish Temple. A resemblance between his design and the Dome of the Rock in Jerusalem, which was often conflated with the temple, has often been noticed. Bramante incorporated various references to the temple into what is generally assumed to be his definitive design for St Peter's. The number of doors – twelve – echoed the number of gates into the Heavenly Jerusalem of St John and St Augustine, the mystical city and the rebuilt temple being seen as more or less the same thing. A drawing for an olive-leaf capital seems to follow biblical accounts of Solomon's temple, with its rich vegetable ornament. One might also notice a hint of the greatest domed construction in the Byzantine tradition, Justinian's sixth-century church of Hagia Sophia in Constantinople, modern Istanbul. Proverbially, that emperor exclaimed, 'Solomon, I have outdone you!' when he saw his architects' creation, and it is not difficult to imagine how keenly Julius II looked forward to making such a boast about Justinian. Indeed, the windy, allegorising rhetoric of Julius's court surpassed the best efforts of Nicholas V's chronicler Gianozzo Manetti. Egidio or Giles of Viterbo, Julius's personal preacher, found time to compare the Pope to Solomon (and his uncle, Sixtus IV, to David), Justinian, Augustus and even the pagan god Janus, the guarantor of peace in ancient Rome, and the titular deity of the Janiculum hill.

Bramante's plan (Fig. 7) doesn't precisely correspond to descriptions either of Solomon's temple or Herod's successor to it, although it does somewhat resemble a squared-off and slightly elaborated version of Hagia Sophia. But it is very much in the Italian Renaissance tradition of formal purity, centralised forms – the circle, square and Greek cross – and an awareness of perspectival effects (the first Italian to paint pictures which conformed to the laws of linear perspective, the Florentine Filippo Brunelleschi, went on to find fame as an architect). But the new church was not built on a *tabula rasa* like the Tempietto. The ground beneath it was soft. It was surrounded by buildings. Its scale was apparently determined by the alterations begun under Nicholas V half a century before (though we don't know how far these got). The choir or tribune for which foundations had been dug perhaps as early as the 1450s gave a definitive westward boundary for the church. The purported tomb of St Peter, which had not been significantly disturbed for more than 1,000 years, formed a roughly central marker. The east-facing wing of Bramante's design – the nearest this centralised conception got to a 'nave' – was never built, but was probably intended to mirror the tribune to the west, although recent scholarship has mooted a less aggressive design, also by Bramante, from early in 1506; this would have followed Nicholas V's policy of remodelling the western part of the church while leaving the Early Christian nave largely intact. Certainly the old nave was left largely untouched during the first phase of rebuilding, and for around a century afterwards.

From 1506 work began. The apse and transepts of Old St Peter's, and the western end of its nave, were knocked down, and the new church began to rise. Huddled in the sprouting masonry of his new basilica, Bramante built a little house over the shrine of St Peter, the tegurium, to protect the apostle's remains from the builders' enthusiasm. It was a stout, pedimented rectangle, with Tuscan columns set into its walls. The semicircular apse of the fourth-century church was retained as its back wall. It has been suggested that this was to be a permanent arrangement. If so, it might have headed off those critics who felt there was something blasphemous about demolishing the Constantinian basilica. Somewhat unrealistically, Julius vetoed any removal of material from the old church, while Bramante tended to get the blame for the traumas it suffered, winning the nickname Ruinante from one papal official. The tegurium, together with the Constantinian fragment behind it, and, more particularly, the tomb which proverbially lay beneath it, would serve as a metaphorical substitute for the larger, demolished whole, an architectural counterpart to the Catholic practice of hoarding and venerating relics. Nevertheless, arguments about the rights and wrongs of demolition would continue to hang over the rebuilding project for the next, troubled century.

Bramante died in 1514, a year after Julius. At this point the western end of the old church was gone and the four main crossing piers of the new one were in place, with four delicate arches threaded between them. Some work had begun elsewhere. Confusingly, the choir, the western wing of the new church, was more or less finished – but not quite to Bramante's design. Later drawings of St Peter's under construction show something much more like the original project of Nicholas V, which Julius II had considered completing before opting for a more drastic solution. Architectural historians have been much troubled by this. It's one thing to borrow the foundations of an existing building, especially on a slippery site like the Vatican hill, and Bramante's presentation plan seems to have been calculated to do so, but it's quite another to compromise the formal purity of an architectural idea which is all about formal purity. The choir as built by around 1514 simply doesn't quite fit with what we see in Bramante's paper plan, nor with the medal of 1506 which constitutes our only proof of how his church was intended to look from the ground. This curious inconsistency has led some to conclude that the kind of radical, synthetic solution suggested by Bramante's presentation drawings had given way to a more piecemeal approach, whereby the east end and crossing would be remodelled and the old nave retained, its fate to be argued another day. It might just be the case that a substantial start had been made on the choir under Nicholas, and it would have seemed wasteful to demolish it so soon. But, wasteful or not, the choir was demolished, in 1585, under the wrecker Pope Sixtus V.

So it may be that Bramante's plans for St Peter's, as influential as they were on paper, were never really put into practice. Certainly, what he did build was not strong enough to sustain itself – it had already started to split and sag by around 1520, and in 1540, when Sebastiano Serlio illustrated it in the third volume of his architectural treatise along with the antiquities of Rome, he veined his woodcut illustrations of even the unbuilt majority of Bramante's St Peter's with fine lines signifying cracks just as in antique buildings like the Pantheon. His commentary obliquely criticised Bramante for his reckless ambition: 'too much fearlessness comes from presumption, and presumption from knowing little, but ... timidity is an excellent thing, giving one always to believe one knows nothing or little.' This strikes an ironic contrast with Francesco Milizia, 250 years later, for whom Bramante's work was 'dry and timid'.

The next thirty-two years are a bit of a shambles, even if it must be remembered that the authorities had several other pressing claims on their time. Julius's successor, the first Medici Pope Leo X, handed St Peter's over to Raphael, better known as a painter than an architect, but an ally and countryman of Bramante's, and an adopted Florentine (and the designer of a lovely, very Florentine-looking church, Sant'Eligio degli Orefici, just off the Via Giulia across the Tiber from St Peter's). Also involved at this point were Fra Giocondo – as much a theoretician as a practitioner of architecture – though he had built a bridge in Paris, so maybe was brought in to advise on the special difficulties presented by the soft, wet ground under St Peter's – and Giuliano da Sangallo, who had already tinkered around on the church under the Venetian Pope Paul II in the late fifteenth century, and had been one of Bramante's rivals in the run-up to 1506. As of 1516 Antonio da Sangallo, Giuliano's nephew, and a former assistant to Bramante and Raphael, was also on the payroll. Before his death in 1520, Raphael found time to put forward a modification of Bramante's plan (though some people say he simply dusted off an alternative plan devised by Bramante himself). This proposed a Latin cross, with one long arm – the nave – and three short ones in preference to Bramante's more geometrically resonant Greek cross, which had set four arms of equal length into a square with a hemispherical dome at the exact centre. A design attributed to Fra Giocondo also survives, for a rectangular church with a large apse on the western end, containing several direct references to the Basilica of Maxentius. Despite the wagonload of surviving drawings which pertain to this period in the church's reconstruction, it is difficult to know what to make of this apparent volte-face. It has been argued that the contras in the

[73]

demolition debate had temporarily prevailed, and that some sort of fusion of Bramante's design with the old nave was now being discussed. Equally likely is the scenario that the idealism and innovation of St Peter's Version 2.0 had – again, temporarily – given way to some more pragmatic demands about capacity and ease of use.

Some kind of wider anxiety about the relationship between religious practice and architectural form may also have begun to make itself felt around this time. When Julius had his medal struck in 1506, nobody would have thought of St Peter's, old or new, as a 'Catholic' building, simply a Christian one. References to prototypes in Byzantium and Palestine may even have been partly intended to reflect the ecumenical outlook which had been so strong in the mid-fifteenth century, and the *entente cordiale* which the Western and Eastern churches had achieved at the Council of Florence. But things quickly changed. In 1510, an Augustinian friar from what would one day be Germany was going through the prescribed motions on a pilgrimage to Rome, hauling himself up the Holy Staircase next to St John Lateran on his knees, wishing his parents were dead so he could use his observances to get them out of Purgatory, just as any good Catholic would. Then he had an epiphany of doubt. Who knew, he thought, whether it was so? Meaning, not what if there was no God – Heaven forbid – but what if the mere enactment of certain ordained rituals were not enough to guarantee grace, salvation and admission to the Kingdom of Heaven? How dare we think we know how to win God over, as if he were some soft-hearted schoolmaster who'll let us out of school early in exchange for a big, shiny apple? What, in short, if there were no Purgatory?

The friar's name was Martin Luther, and he was to become the best-known and most reviled religious reformer in the history of the Western Church. Protestantism as preached by Luther, Calvin and others succeeded for many reasons, and it should be remembered that Luther's coarsely chauvinistic attacks on an effete and corrupt Latin church culture probably won him more admirers in chilly Northern Europe than the finer points of his theology. But the two forks of his attack were anyway intricately related. Luther's famous ninety-five theses were provoked by an impressively sleazy deal struck in 1517 between Albert of Brandenburg and Pope Leo X. Albert bought the archbishopric of Mainz with 10,000 ducats borrowed from the Fugger bank; Leo gave him permission to sell indulgences, documents entitling named individuals to what amounted to parole from Purgatory, the issuing of which has been generally frowned upon in Christian history (Dante has a special place reserved for 'simoniacs' – sellers of indulgences – in his *Inferno*). Half the proceeds would go to pay off the Fuggers and half towards the rebuilding of St Peter's. Luther wrote: 'The revenues of all Christendom are being sucked into this insatiable basilica. The Germans laugh at calling this the common treasure of Christendom.' This only slightly concealed appeal to raw nationalism gives us a clear glimpse of Luther the politician (certainly he had nothing to say about Latin or Greek crosses). But the Church was in manifest need of ethical and constitutional reform at the time, and New St Peter's, bloated and extravagant, its construction indecisively and incautiously overseen, made a perfect exhibit for the prosecution. Leo is supposed to have said that Luther would 'feel different when sober', incidentally.

[75]

Luther's revolution cost the True Church dear in lost territories and broken alliances. But it is important to remember that things had not been particularly rosy before he arrived, nor would they be entirely bleak in future. The temporal power of the papacy had been under threat since the Middle Ages; Popes had been swept up in (or, in several cases, had actively instigated) the wars which raged through Italy from the late fifteenth century onwards. A bitter betrayal by the Habsburg Emperor Charles V would lead in 1527 to the disastrous Sack of Rome, and a humiliating redrawing of the balance of power between Caesar and God. But the Catholic Church landed, catlike, on its feet. As the preferred spiritual partner of the Spanish branch of the Habsburg Empire, the Church soon enjoyed unrivalled access to literally millions of fresh souls, whom a little education and the occasional crack of the whip might soon rid of their pagan beliefs. Organisations like Ignatius of Loyola's Society of Jesus took a newly pragmatic approach to doctrine and helped the Spanish and Portuguese build vast empires across the Atlantic and in the Indies. Slaves, spices, tobacco, mahogany, blue Brazilian marbles and tons of gold went a good way towards easing Roman pain at the loss of a few drizzly tracts of Northern Europe to the Protestant heresy.

Nevertheless, it is really in the more stringent reaches of Protestantism that we first encounter two related complaints about Catholic culture which would reverberate through the sixteenth century, and have done so intermittently ever since. Lutherans and Calvinists dusted off an argument last seen in the Iconoclastic controversy which had afflicted the Orthodox religion some 700 years before. Religious art was not only proof of the vanity and extravagance of the Roman

Church; it was also by its very nature idolatrous. If you painted a picture of Jesus and planted it on top of an altar, then you were praying to the image rather than the divinity, a clear breach of the second commandment. Coupled with a new insistence on the kinship between material poverty and spiritual wealth (a convenient belief for any underdog to hold – and one which had worked nicely for the Early Christians, of course), this led to the stripping and whitewashing of hundreds of churches, and the destruction of thousands of works of art, all under the guise of reform.

In 1563 the Catholic Church would finally respond to all this in the Acts of the Council of Trent, a supposedly ecumenical think-tank convened by the Farnese Pope Paul III, which sat twenty-five times over a period of eighteen years. Most of the Council's conclusions were either doctrinal or, as it were, managerial, with the *index librorum prohibitorum* established and the Inquisition given new powers. Standard accounts of Western art history also set out the way in which the Council would affect religious art in years to come: the stomach-turning martyrdoms, trembling ecstasies and Immaculate Conceptions, the theatricalised ritual of Mass, the Latin-cross church as an embracing symbol of the crucified Christ. It all seems shrewdly calculated to deliver a feast for the senses and the very nerve-endings, next to which the introspective and ascetic nature of Protestant worship would seem to a wavering worshipper like pretty thin gruel. But the idea of a coherent artistic response to the trauma of the Reformation needs to be put forward with caution; certainly, such a response took a while to appear.

The solid conservatism of the Council's conclusions on religious art – no nudity, no divergence from biblical sources,

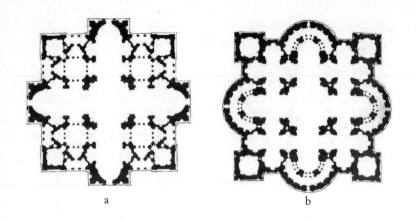

a

b

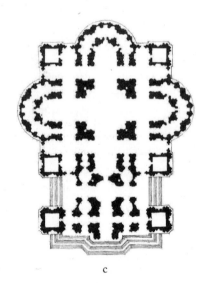

c

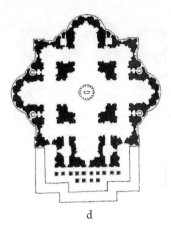

d

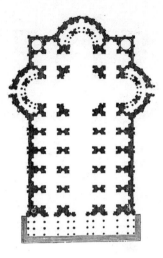

e

7. Plans of St Peter's, by (a) Bramante (1506), (b) Peruzzi (around 1514), (c) Sangallo (1539), (d) Michelangelo (1546) and (e) Raphael (around 1514). These are the most well-known proposals for the rebuilding of the basilica, though others were certainly put forward, by Bramante and others. Raphael's design tacks a nave onto a version of Bramante's 1506 template – he may have got this idea from Bramante.

easy on the classical imagery and, crucially, no more funny-shaped churches – would be a significant influence on the final phase of rebuilding at St Peter's early in the seventeenth century, and on its decoration forty-odd years after that. During the sixteenth century the picture was murkier. The Renaissance's open-minded intellectual engagement with classical thought and art (a tradition by no means as easy as many Renaissance humanists made it look to reconcile with Christianity in either its metaphysics or its ethics) came to a sudden end. It is convenient to date the extinction to the Sack of Rome, an event which the religious were quick to read as divine retribution, a delayed millenarian catastrophe and a Godly rebuke for worldliness and crypto-paganism (though this attitude might itself have been a Christian trope on the sack of Rome by Alaric in the fifth century CE, which had prompted Augustine to write *City of God*). But even before 1527, the writing was on the wall. A centrally planned and overtly Roman-looking St Peter's might have provoked all sorts of anxieties simply because it didn't really look like a church at all, but rather resembled some kind of hybrid of temple and bath-house.

Whether the product of religious conservatism or practical exigency, Raphael's Latin-cross design was disregarded by the next Capomaestro, the Sienese painter and architect Baldassare Peruzzi. Peruzzi reverted to a slightly beefier version of Bramante's plan, which was incorporated into rebuilding from around 1520 (Fig. 7). Peruzzi also found time to devise a Latin-cross plan, so clearly had no deep ideological commitment to Bramante's High Renaissance purism. Work proceeded slowly. There were problems about money, and – it seems – the stability of Bramante's design (so it may be that all Peruzzi wanted to do was return to the 1506 plan, but enhance its stability). Clement VII, the bastard Medici Pope, set up a new bureaucratic tier, the Congregation of the Reverend Fabric of St Peter's (the organisation which still looks after the basilica today). By the time of the Sack, the half-built basilica had acquired the appearance of a ruin, sprouting vegetation, its form jagged and disrupted, its raw rubble, brick and concrete substance exposed.

This is how it was seen by a group of Netherlandish artists working in Rome during the 1520s and 1530s. In a city filled with ruins, here was a new building with all the tragic grandeur of an ancient one. Its many classical references now had a piquant directness, as it seemed to be in the same state as the antiquities it sought to imitate. Its parlous physique gave it a paradoxical aura of greatness, a bloody-but-unbowed quality, as if it had withstood the depredations of Attila the Hun rather than just Charles V's mercenaries (Bramante's tegurium had kept the rampaging soldiers clear of Peter's tomb, though several relics from St Peter's were looted and paraded in the streets). Later in the century, when work was going on again but the church remained unfinished, its status as an honorary ruin would be exploited by Roman printmakers, who would create deliberate visual rhymes in their views of the city whereby the cylindrical drum on top of St Peter's, built in the 1560s but without its crowning dome until the end of the century, would lead the eye in a straight line across Rome, linking St Peter's with the Colosseum, in the middle of town, and the Amphitheatrum Castrense next to Santa Croce in Gerusalemme, in the south-east corner.

The next stage in the rebuilding imbroglio came in 1536, two years after the death of Clement VII. By now the principal architect was Antonio da Sangallo. Antonio came up with a couple of variants on the Bramante–Raphael formula, then spent the years 1539 to 1545, in collaboration with Antonio Labacco, crafting a vast (around eight metres long) and notoriously expensive model of his definitive design. Antonio's design takes Bramante as its starting point, and adheres rigidly to classical principles of structure and ornament, but nevertheless manages to look decidedly odd. The four corners of Bramante's Greek cross are topped with stubby octagonal lanterns. Bramante's Pantheonish dome is endowed with two circular arcades, one wider than the other, running round its base. The Gordian knot of centralised planning versus a long nave is sliced by placing a single, domed bay to the east of the church, then setting a wide façade crowned with two towers beyond that, as if a conventional long-naved church had been cinched into a corset (120 years later, Christopher Wren would do something similar in his unexecuted Great Model design for St Paul's Cathedral in London).

At this point the mighty Michelangelo lumbered into the debate for the first time. *Persona non grata* in Florence after backing an anti-Medici uprising, he returned to Rome in 1533, and prior to the Sangallo model's unveiling had recently finished his masterly fresco of the *Last Judgement* in the Sistine Chapel. The picture has been widely interpreted as a metaphorical lamentation over the Sack of Rome, though the *Fall of the Rebel Angels* possibly planned for the space before 1527 would hardly have been the most lighthearted of subjects.

Michelangelo's biographers have fallen over themselves to portray him as aloof and solitary, brooding over the mysteries of art and spirituality, far from mundane reality. But he seems to have spent most of his adult life getting violent crushes on some people and falling into bitter feuds with others. Attacked by the poet Pietro Aretino and the master of ceremonies Biagio da Cesena for the nudity in the *Last Judgement* (another example of how even Catholics were getting stricter about religious proprieties during this period), he is said to have painted them both into the picture – and not among the numinous saved, either. His biggest cheerleader, the writer and courtier Giorgio Vasari, was also a painter, though in truth a middling one. In 1546, when Vasari proudly told Michelangelo that he'd finished a cycle of frescoes in the Palazzo della Cancelleria in just 100 days, Michelangelo's laconic response was, 'So I see.' Vasari, incidentally, had depicted Pope Paul III as Zerubbabel, the architect of the second Jewish Temple and the successor to Solomon, in the same cycle.

Michelangelo is said to have attacked Antonio da Sangallo's model not only on the grounds of taste but also because it had been needlessly elaborate and expensive (in a few years' time his own model for the dome would be a much more low-key affair). Vasari quotes him using the phrase *opera tedesca*, German work. What Michelangelo meant was that the tall towers and bristling pinnacles of the model suggested the silhouette of a Gothic building rather than the crisply delineated volumes of a classical one – a stinging insult for the rigorous classicist Antonio. Whether or not this was meant as a job application, it was certainly interpreted as one. In 1546, overcome by age and disease while working on a canal outside Rome, Antonio died. Pope Paul III briskly overrode Michelangelo's elaborate protestations of unworthiness and appointed him the latest, though not the last, architect of St Peter's.

4

....

ELABORATIONS

If you don't break the rules every so often you'll never transcend them.

Gian Lorenzo Bernini

One of the puzzles surrounding Michelangelo's work on St Peter's is that nobody is quite sure how much of it was done by Michelangelo. He was already seventy-one when he took Paul III's shilling, and most of what he began wasn't finished until twenty or more years after his death. To see those parts of the church which look most 'Michelangelesque' you really have to be outside, looking at the dome from the Ponte Sant'Angelo, the Aventine hill or the Janiculum, or at the strange, saurian back and side elevations of the building from within the Vatican gardens themselves (see Chapter 7, and 'Planning a Visit?' on page 215). But the fact that these portions look as they do may just reflect the old proverb about imitation and flattery. That the different elements of the church seem to hang together as well as they do speaks of a remarkable and drawn-out collaboration between individuals across more than two centuries, from the paper dreams initiated under Nicholas V to the decoration of the interior in the mid-seventeenth century.

Michelangelo's design for St Peter's reverted to Bramante's

Greek cross ('Whoever departs from Bramante departs from the truth,' he said, gnomically). But he made the four main crossing piers, the structural backbone of the church, broader and sturdier and, crucially, thickened and stabilised the outer walls, creating heavy prisms of masonry to buttress the dome, and wrapping the exterior in dense bunches of overlapping pilasters (Francesco Milizia, a strict classicist, and a rare exception to the admiring chorus which has generally attended on Michelangelo's work, wrote at the end of the eighteenth century that he had 'folded and refolded [them] round the outside in a most distasteful way'). The lightness and transparency which Bramante's plan might have brought, and the spatial complexity which Antonio da Sangallo's reworking of that plan had promised, gave way to a flat-footed monumentality, decidedly Roman in spirit – but enlivened by a sculptor's eye, or feel, for architectural detail. But there's the rub. Michelangelo has been consistently identified – Milizia notwithstanding – by critics and art historians as possessing that rare attribute 'genius', an attribute which consists, among other things, in an all but infinite capacity for not dying. A genius is generally presumed to have a 'late' style in which the passionate creative surges of youth take on some sort of autumnal hue. Images of Michelangelo's conception of St Peter's are rare, but they tend to show something a little more austere than what one sees in surviving parts of his exterior today. For example, it seems that he planned a row of plain, arched openings to run round the outside walls of the church up near the roof. The heavily ornamented rectangular windows which were installed instead were probably devised by younger colleagues either as a sincere attempt to fulfil what the *capo* would have wanted, or, more intriguingly, as an attempt at something closer to what his clients had been expecting from him than what he came up with in the event – something more in keeping with the artist's brand, and less with his evolving personal vision. So there's very little Michelangelo on show at St Peter's; and what little there is may be a kind of well-intentioned architectural forgery.

Meanwhile, the efforts of his seventeenth-century successors mean that the interior of the church is more or less devoid of any trace of Michelangelo. There's his *Pietà*, of course, a survivor from Old St Peter's, and the dome (though as vast as this may be it isn't as distinctive inside as outside); and a cramped-looking pediment above some of the windows which the keen *michelangelista* might just about identify as by the master's hand. Certainly, the great void under the dome gives an intense vertical drama to the basilica's interior. It unmistakably signals the most important part of the church, the area over the so-called *confessio*, a sort of indoor grotto which curves down towards to the holy of holies, the site of Peter's tomb. Walking along the nave floor, pacing out the basilica's prodigious length, ticking off each of the vanquished rivals commemorated in the marble pavement, there is a powerful sense of crescendo (Fig. 8). Yet for this we have to thank not Michelangelo, who wanted a smaller, neater, less ornamented and proportionately taller-seeming space: nor Maderno, whose nave was added for pragmatic reasons as much as aesthetic ones; but the real presiding genius of New St Peter's, Gian Lorenzo Bernini, who understood the paradox that in order to make people intensely aware of an empty space you have to put something in it.

We have seen how the authorities dithered over whether to make New St Peter's a centralised space somewhat shorter

8. Interior of St Peter's, by Piranesi, from *Vedute di Roma*, mid-seventeenth century. Here Piranesi shows his familiarity with the scene-painting tradition perfected by the Bibiena family and others in his native Venice. The shooting perspective exaggerates the scale of the church, as do the tiny figures.

than its Early Christian forebear, or a long rectangle or Latin cross which would occupy the footprint of Constantine's basilica more precisely. As of the turn of the seventeenth century, St Peter's was an untidy bricolage, half 'old', half 'new'. There were essentially two fragments or ruins of churches standing cheek-by-jowl on the site. Michelangelo's design still lacked a façade, while about half the nave of the original church remained doggedly in its original position. The two structures were separated by Antonio da Sangallo's *muro divisorio* or dividing wall, built more than sixty years before. A fresco in the Vatican library depicts Michelangelo's projected façade, in full unencumbered view, framed by a neat, imaginary piazza. The dome is easier to see without a long nave and wide façade in the way, and Michelangelo's compact plan is clearly visible. The simple temple-like façade in the fresco makes direct reference to the Pantheon, always a key reference point for St Peter's. The ensemble looks fine enough, but it would have been impossible to realise without demolishing the Sistine Chapel, the Pauline Chapel, the Raphael Stanze and loggia, and generally playing havoc with the Vatican palace hard by the basilica: none of which was ever going to happen.

The fact that in 1606 Paul V finally opted for demolition of the old church and elongation of the new one should probably be seen in terms of practical and liturgical considerations rather than aesthetic ones: the need for a large space to accommodate a large congregation and the post-Tridentine insistence on traditional church architecture, coupled with the Church's new emphasis on a conspicuous, not to say theatrical, performance of Mass. Maderno's nave of 1607–14 allowed for six new side-chapels to augment the two already built by Della Porta a couple of decades before, enhancing the practical usefulness of the building by enabling different things to go on in different places at the same time. It permitted opponents of the demolition of Old St Peter's to believe that the new church somehow encompassed the old, as Bramante's tegurium had 'encompassed' Peter's shrine a century before. This wasn't literally true, of course, but it is striking that the crypt or so-called Grottoes beneath the new church have a floor level only slightly lower than did the nave of the old one, and it is into these Grottoes that most of the displaced tombs from the old church were reinserted. So one could just about imagine that the illustrious dead had only been disturbed momentarily before being restored to something fairly close to their previous resting-place.

The new nave also conveniently, if a shade clumsily, forged a link between the church and the Vatican palace. The benediction loggia which ran across the façade of St Peter's at first-floor level connected at its northern edge with the Sala Regia, an ambassadorial reception room, and the Pauline Chapel, built for Paul's namesake Paul III and decorated by Michelangelo, among others (you can see the window of the Pauline Chapel when you queue for the dome climb or – currently – the Grottoes). Extending St Peter's eastwards until its façade was roughly level with the Sala Regia was an easy way to integrate the Pope's church and the papal palace next door, whereas more radical proposals like Bramante's or Michelangelo's would have created awkward gaps and juxtapositions which only demolishing parts of the Vatican palace could really have solved. But however you look at it, Paul's policy at St Peter's was conservative in nature. The inventiveness and utopianism of the Renaissance had given way to something more pragmatic, not to say mundane. New St Peter's as built was a very much more unremarkable church than most of its unrealised earlier avatars. This has usually been blamed on the architect who built the nave and façade, rather than on the papal officials who turned their backs on a century of intermittent brilliance and enduring muddle, and elected to concern themselves solely with the art of the possible.

Carlo Maderno was born in 1556, in what was then Lombardy and is now Switzerland. He was involved in the Roman churchbuilding boom of the late 1580s and 90s, designing the façade of Santa Susanna, now the American church in Rome, and the dome of Sant'Andrea della Valle, an ingenious, slimmed-down variant on Michelangelo's dome at St Peter's. In place of the austere architecture of his uncle Domenico Fontana, under whom he worked at the Vatican before becoming architect of St Peter's in 1603, Maderno developed a monumental but decorative style which would be hugely influential in Rome and beyond for a century or more. His work at St Peter's is in many ways uncharacteristic, as it effectively amounts to a pastiche of Michelangelo. The fact that he didn't assert a style of his own more forcefully in the face of his illustrious predecessor doesn't necessarily make him a 'weak' architect, to adapt the literary critic Harold Bloom's notion of a 'weak' poet, swept along by tradition; indeed, at Sant'Andrea he adapted Michelangelo's dome from St Peter's in an innovative and forceful way. Architecture in most cases is a pragmatic and collaborative art, especially at so sensitive a site as St Peter's. Indeed, Maderno's nave transformed the basilica, emphasising the horizontal element of a newly expanded space, accentuating the role of perspective in the visitor's apprehension of the church, and providing abundant wall and ceiling space for later decorators to fill. He also cleverly if not quite invisibly dealt with the misaligned obelisk outside in the piazza (see Chapter 1).

Still, the result of distending the eastern arm of Michelangelo's Greek cross with Maderno's nave was in one sense to make the interior of St Peter's seem ordinary, if extraordinarily large. Certainly it is now difficult to spot which elements of the church are by whom, and which date from when. Having mostly been decorated by Bernini, the interior of the church looks almost generically seventeenth century, the age of the Baroque in Europe: colourful, exuberant architecture, extensively adorned with sculpted figures of wild demeanour, clothed in rippling drapery – a frankly luxurious and even oddly sensual effect. The style was Catholic Rome's most influential gift to the world, a bold series of elaborations on the classical tradition as codified during the preceding Renaissance. The word 'baroque' denotes deformity – it's still used by jewellers to describe misshapen pearls – and like many other art-historical terms (Gothic, Impressionist, Fauve and so on) it was coined by detractors rather than admirers of the style. For those who preferred the austere lucidity of 'pure' classicism, the emphasis laid on colour, movement and decoration by Bernini, Borromini and Pietro da Cortona in Rome, and their artistic apostles across Europe, was morally as well as aesthetically dubious. Traditional art history views the Roman Baroque as an expression of resurgent Catholic self-confidence after the first anxieties of the Counter-Reformation, and notes how readily would-be Caesars like Louis XIV of France adapted it to purely secular ends, the celebration of material wealth and political clout. It's a story which is still widely told, though it tends to make individual artists and patrons seem like mere conduits for impersonal, historical forces (and it can make dissenters like Caravaggio or Poussin seem more inexplicable or prodigious than they perhaps were). But in an ecclesiastical context, the prime task of the Baroque was plain: to give concrete expression to the miraculous. Bernini's St Peter's would be a theatre of the divine.

Gian Lorenzo Bernini was born in Naples in 1598. His father, Pietro, was a Florentine sculptor, who brought his family to Rome ten years later. In a standard trope of art-historical biography, the precocious talent of the son quickly eclipsed the father. A funerary bust in the church of Santa Prassede near Santa Maria Maggiore was purportedly carved by Bernini junior at the age of just thirteen (some biographers say ten); by his early twenties he was already a favourite sculptor of the prodigal Cardinal Scipione Borghese, Paul V's nephew. Gian Lorenzo's involvement with St Peter's began in 1624, twelve years after the new nave was finished, and the church occupied him off and on for the rest of his life. His contribution to the interior of the basilica is manifold: sculpted decoration, tombs, enhancements to the floor and nave arcades, and, most conspicuously, two enormous bronze structures, one nestling in the western apse of the church like a giant glittering fungus, one standing a few feet west of the central crossing, beneath the dome and above the apostle's tomb. The former is the Cathedra Petri, arguably the most important reliquary in St Peter's, an elaborate sculptural assembly which sets the four Doctors of the Church at the four corners of an elaborate throne (Fig. 9). In front stand St Ambrose and St Augustine, representing the Latin Church:

9. Cathedra Petri by Bernini, 1657–66. The chair borne aloft by the four Doctors of the Church is in fact a casket for a smaller, simpler and much older chair.

behind, St John Chrysostom and St Anastasius, representing the Greek. The central group is framed by flickering cherubs and apparently lit by gilt-bronze rods radiating from an oval window decorated with the Holy Spirit in the form of a dove. Tobias Smollett was characteristically trenchant about the arrangement in his 1766 *Travels through France and Italy*: '... no more than a heap of puerile finery, better adapted to an Indian pagod, than to a temple built upon the principles of Greek architecture'. In the following century, John Ruskin found Bernini's exuberance almost obscene: 'it is impossible for false taste and base feeling to sink lower'. But neither these nor other detractors' best efforts can diminish the ensemble's barnstorming impact.

The reliquary is an overblown, bombastic counterpart to the relic it contains: a little timber and ivory chair, conventionally regarded as Peter's original throne until it was dated to the Carolingian period (though the timber parts may be older). This is the most emphatic demonstration of papal authority in the whole church. More than the *rota* and the kingliest of the papal tombs, the chair symbolises apostolic succession and the Popes' right to the ear of the faithful. A statement made *ex cathedra* is one which carries the full pomp of the papal office (the doctrine of papal infallibility, agreed at the First Vatican Council in 1870, only applies to such statements). The old wooden relic was once allegedly used by Popes as part of the ceremonial *sedia gestatoria*, a kind of sedan chair, though it hadn't seen active service for centuries when Bernini came to design the Cathedra. Bernini's arrangement achieves many things. It exemplifies as well as any single project could the Roman High Baroque style (that 'High' itself a product of the art-historical model noted above, implying that artistic styles have a kind of organic cycle of growth, maturation and decline). It makes a triumphant statement about the importance of relics in Catholic worship, and a parallel point about St Peter's as a giant reliquary of itself, a monument to its own unfolding history. But the entombing of something which used to be sat on within something which was only meant to be looked at also illustrates a characteristic historical process widely in evidence at St Peter's. Like the *rota*, Peter's chair is a once-functional object repackaged as a decorative one, and as such, its loud exclamations of glory do not quite drown out a whispered rumour of decline.

Alexander VII, the Pope who commissioned the Cathedra Petri in 1657, was much preoccupied by the dwindling political clout of his office. He had been present at the drafting of the Peace of Westphalia, which brought the Thirty Years War to a notional end in 1648, but had refused to sign because of the notorious phrase *cuius regio, eius religio*, which gave the temporal ruler of any given statelet the right to determine the religious practices of all his subjects if he chose. This meant greater religious freedom in some parts of Europe, but less in others. The Habsburg lands became solidly Catholic for a century to come, and education there was passed over to the Jesuits – energetic patrons of Baroque architecture, incidentally – almost wholesale. So in fact the True Church didn't do too badly out of the whole business. Still, taking Peter's real chair out of active service and hiding it away in Bernini's spectacular reliquary might be seen as another example of Alexander's rueful awareness that Rome's future was as a tourist centre rather than a centre of power. The inclusion of figures associated with Orthodox as well as Catholic

Christianity might even be read less as the bold ecumenical declaration which it purported to be than as a decorative conceit to hang from this most ornamental of structures: a kind of Orientalist caprice.

Catholic worship has tended to become more puritanical over the past century or so. The richly metaphorical and sensual approach followed by artists who served the Counter-Reformation has fallen a little out of fashion. There seems to the modern observer to be little of the spiritual about Bernini's chair. Yet one of the objects it resembles most closely – and most unexpectedly – is a monstrance, a decorative frame used to display the Host, the holy bread or wafer, during Mass. Monstrances are usually no more than a couple of feet high: big enough to be visible by the congregation, small enough to stand neatly on an altar. The comparison thus entails one of those wild, lurching contrasts of scale so often seen at St Peter's; but it bears examination nonetheless. Monstrances were a characteristic form in Catholic Baroque decorative art, growing bigger and more elaborate during the seventeenth and early eighteenth centuries (as if organic forces really were at work within them, rather than just the historical metaphor noted above). The doctrine of transubstantiation, the belief that the Host doesn't just symbolise the body of Christ but is truly transformed into it during the Eucharistic ritual (see Chapter 1), was a notion which Protestantism found hard to swallow, so to speak. The post-Tridentine Catholic triumphalism of the seventeenth century promoted Mass not just as a spectacle, but also because it demanded a particular order of belief from those who celebrated it, enabling them to distinguish themselves from the heretics of the North.

The primary focus of Bernini's reliquary is not the chair

itself, but the window above it: a dove, symbol of the Holy Spirit, in stained glass. Light from the window is drawn along the gilt-bronze rods which frame the oval window (especially during the evening, when the sun is in the west). This explosion of forms from a central ellipse is technically called a Glory, and is a common if not quite a ubiquitous feature of monstrances from the seventeenth and early eighteenth centuries. And while the bird in the middle isn't specifically to do with the Eucharist, the emblem of the Holy Spirit does express pretty well the *mysterium fidei*, the mystery of faith, invoked in the Eucharistic ritual (this was the title given to a papal encyclical confirming the doctrine of transubstantiation as recently as the 1960s). Certainly doves hover over many representations of the Eucharist in religious art: for example, in Raphael's famous fresco of the *Disputa* in the Stanza della Segnatura just next to St Peter's in the Vatican palace – a composition, incidentally, which strongly echoes the western end of Constantine's original basilica, with the apostles grouped around Christ in a semicircle as the clergy sat in the apse of Old St Peter's, and the upper part of the fresco gilded, evoking the church's mosaic decoration. To the believer, the Eucharist is not an allegory: it is what it is. Such a believer might not need to 'believe' in allegory at all. Maybe faith can make Bernini's bronze extravaganza into something truthful and incarnate, a glimpse of the divine hovering impossibly but irrefutably in the apse of St Peter's.

As well as what it tells us about papal identity and Catholic belief, the Cathedra Petri also reveals Bernini's uniquely architectural conception of sculpture, not to mention his highly sculptural conception of architecture. Seen up close, the chair and its fluttering attendants seem a little preposterous, if undeniably spectacular. To borrow an unkind phrase used of the Skylon, Misha Black's 'vertical feature' which decorated the Festival of Britain in 1951, the Cathedra is a vast, inflated structure with no visible means of support. The chair is cantilevered out from the back wall of the church, and the saints do not touch it directly. There are a few too many cherubs. The bronze clouds look nothing like clouds. James Lees-Milne wrote that the gilt-bronze beams radiating from the west window were 'planks soused in gold semolina pudding'. The ensemble's origins in the mostly vanished world of temporary or festival architecture seem only too plain. But the really clever thing Bernini did with this, one of his later sculptural commissions at St Peter's, was to make it clarify and animate the greater spatial drama of the basilica. One's first glimpse of the chair is likely to be from the nave, framed by the four twisted, leaf-flecked bronze columns which constitute the dominant central element of the basilica, Bernini's first major commission there, the canopy over the papal altar and Peter's tomb conventionally known as the baldacchino (Fig. 10).

⧗

The papal altar at St Peter's – not to be confused with the 'high' altar, which sits in the western apse just in front of the Cathedra – is relatively little used, since only the Pope or his appointed substitute can celebrate Mass there (during John Paul II's last illness, it was Joseph Ratzinger who deputised for him at Easter, a sure sign of anointment to the keen student of papal intrigue). The main spiritual business of the church is conducted elsewhere: in the confessionals, each one specifying the languages spoken within like a string of Parisian restaurants; around the subsidiary altars where particular saints may be asked to intercede in specific cases or on particular days; and in the side-chapels. Most of the time, the importance of the papal altar is essentially visual or navigational. It marks the intersection of the basilica's three cardinal axes: the vertical, from dome to *confessio* and tomb; the lateral, from one transept to another, and the orthogonal, from the central door at the eastern end of the church to the apse opposite. It also serves as a further witness to the long historical trajectory of St Peter's, as it is cannibalised from antique materials – a collection of watery-white Proconnesian marble slabs excavated from the Forum of Nerva under Pope Clement VIII in 1594.

It was not so much as an ornamental canopy for the altar that the baldacchino was intended, though its decoration echoes a cloth canopy which was held over the *sedia gestatoria*, so some sort of direct personal reference to the Pope should probably be inferred. But the baldacchino also indicates and celebrates the very first Pope, who happens to be buried beneath it. The precise location of Peter's tomb would still be unknown for more than three centuries after the baldacchino was installed; but the sixteenth-century papal altar had been built on an earlier structure, which itself surrounded the original Constantinian shrine, so there was a chain of belief about where the tomb was. Still, just a few feet in any direction and the tomb discovered and hailed as Peter's in the mid-twentieth century would have been obliterated by the foundations of Bernini's baldacchino, which wrought plenty of havoc beneath the basilica as it was.

The monument consists of four bronze columns on

carved marble bases, each one topped by an angel, with four bronze scrolls converging diagonally to make a flamelike peak over the centre. This in turn is capped by an orb and a crucifix. The columns are based on the so-called 'Solomonic' columns which had formed a not dissimilar structure at the west end of Old St Peter's, and which were thought to be authentic relics of the sacked Temple of Jerusalem (Bernini moved eight of these up into the corner piers of the crossing, where they frame four sculptural reliefs). Bernini's use of bronze, which generated all sorts of technical difficulties on this huge scale, may also have been meant to evoke biblical descriptions of the Temple, as may the olive and laurel leaves he modelled on the columns. Or the metallic medium may have been a signal that this canopy was not to be judged as a piece of architecture, but as an essay in some different art: sculpture, or even what we would call ecclesiastical furniture. If so, it didn't work. The baldacchino was criticised as a chimera – a hybrid of incompatible elements (for reasons which would strike most fairminded observers as insufferably pedantic) – and a Gothicism, because of its ogival top. The neoclassical architect John Soane called it a 'lasting reproach to Bernini's memory'; Dickens thought it looked like a bedstead. Others have at least praised its huge height – about the same as the Palazzo Farnese across the river, it is conventionally alleged.

It did not help that the bronze for the baldacchino was popularly supposed to have been stripped from the portico of the best-loved and best-preserved antique building in the city, the very temple which had cast such a long shadow over the rebuilding of St Peter's: the Pantheon. There were several precedents for the re-use of antique materials in modern projects. Paul III had melted down a hoard of Etruscan bronze from Tarquinia and used it to decorate St John Lateran, while the arch-moderniser Sixtus V destroyed the Septizodium or Septizonium, a richly articulated screen of columns near the Circus Maximus (admittedly, in order to restore other antiquities). Two inscriptions flanking the doors of the Pantheon – nice of them to leave those – try to put a positive spin on things, but a certain sheepish note is impossible to overlook. One talks about 'public safety' – the coffering was partly melted down for artillery – as well as the 'ornamentation of the apostolic tomb'; the other points out that the Pantheon had been enhanced with towers, the much-derided *orecchie di asino* or 'donkey's ears' built by Bernini in 1629. Both inscriptions date from 1632, the ninth year of one of the most influential, not to say notorious, pontificates since that of Julius II.

In 1623, Maffeo Barberini became Pope Urban VIII. He came from a branch of an affluent mercantile family from Florence. His clan's original name was Tafani da Barberino, a less than fragrant soubriquet given that a *tafano* is a horsefly. At some stage, perhaps during the family's where-there's-muck-there's-brass phase, horseflies were used as part of its *stemma* or crest. But as the tang of exertion gave way to the sweet smell of success, Maffeo's horseflies underwent a corresponding metamorphosis. For the next twenty-one years bees would swarm all over Rome, in travertine, embroidery and bronze; on fountains and gateways, huddling in church cornices. This was a new Golden Age; Rome was a land of milk and honey; and the constant and conspicuous reminders of its ruling family left no one in any doubt about whom they had to thank. However, the chief characteristics of Urban's regime, as cultured and energetic a patron as he may have been, make one think he might have done better to stick with the horseflies. A warrior Pope on Julius II's model, he poured resources into the pro-Habsburg side in the Thirty Years' War. He also pursued a long and costly war against the small duchy of Mantua, with little to show for it but the remains of Matilda of Canossa, an eleventh-century termagant extracted from San Benedetto Po and entombed in some style in St Peter's.

In between times he indulged in nepotism on a gleeful scale, and imposed swingeing new taxes, including, controversially, a duty on wine. Papa Gabella, 'Taxpope', was one of his many nicknames. His intellectual credentials are slightly tarnished by the fact that Galileo's trial took place on his watch. His despoliation of the Pantheon provoked what is regarded as one of the most memorable pasquinades in history: *quod non fecerunt barbari, fecerunt Barberini* – what the barbarians didn't do the Barberini did. In fact, strictly speaking, this wasn't a pasquinade at all. These were anonymously posted next to Rome's so-called 'talking statues', the best-known of which were two eroded warriors near Piazza Navona, one of whom was baptised Pasquino at the turn of the sixteenth century (and much admired by Bernini in the seventeenth). Pasquino and his comrades became a safe outlet for scurrilous and subversive opinions, a place for the browbeaten *papalini*, the Pope's subjects, to let off rhetorical steam – a function Pasquino at least still serves today. The Barberini gag was made by the Pope's personal physician, one Giulio Mancini; Urban, something of a man of letters himself, was probably in on the joke. That's not to say that Pasquino was silent on Urban's policies. One choice example might serve as an epitaph for his career: *Ingrassò l'api e scorticò l'armento*. He fattened the bees, and skinned the cattle.

Urban VIII lost no time in getting Bernini on the payroll. From 1624 the artist was working on the baldacchino, then on Maderno's death in 1629 he became architect of St Peter's. He would hold the post for the rest of his life, apart from a short flurry of controversy in the early 1640s after one of the bell-towers he designed to 'complete' Maderno's façade – unabashed by the hilarity his 'donkey's ears' at the Pantheon had unleashed a decade or so before – began to subside, and threatened to take the façade with it. During that period rivals were keen to point out that Bernini, despite his undeniable gifts as a sculptor, was not a trained architect. But at this point there was really no such thing as a trained architect, and we have already seen how difficult it was to build on the flood-plain between the Tiber and what remained of the Vatican hill. Bernini was anyway the smoothest of courtly operators, and soon managed to get his feet back under the papal table, though not before he had had to bribe Cardinal Pamphili with a diamond sent to him by Charles I of England's wife Henrietta Maria as a sweetener to try to make him sculpt the king's portrait.

As controversial as it has often been since, it has to be allowed that the baldacchino is finely and knowingly tai-lored to its setting, and to the long history of the site. We do not know how much Bernini knew about Old St Peter's; Constantine's apse was long gone by the time he came to Rome, but the old church was reasonably well documented. Today we have a fairly good idea what the shrine or tomb area inside Constantine's basilica looked like as early as the sixth century CE, thanks to a relief on a Byzantine casket of that date found near Pola in modern Croatia. The twisted or Solomonic columns are there; more strikingly, so is the motif of diagonally intersecting arches, which Bernini seems first to have copied literally in an early design for his baldacchino, then later (if we borrow a term from his detractors) to have Gothicised. In general it is important to remember that he was more exercised by tradition and antique precedent than conventional histories have painted him. Even in the absence of clear documentary evidence, it is entirely plausible to believe that Bernini was trying to evoke the old shrine, but to improve and enlarge it in the process. He was also certainly aware of corresponding structures which stood over the main altars at St John Lateran and San Paolo fuori le Mura: both crowned by spiky Gothic pinnacles, and so both prestigious precedents for the apparent solecism of his own peaked crown at St Peter's. As so often here and elsewhere, one monument is set in conversation with others, both nearby and distant, across both space and time. References to the Temple run parallel with other invocations: of Old St Peter's itself, and of the other great apostolic churches in Rome; of the ever-present Pantheon, even, since its metal was recast in the baldacchino (maybe expropriation, not imitation, is the sincerest form of flattery).

Seventeenth-century art, the art of the Baroque, if that's a useful term, is particularly notable for this richness and plurality of allusion. It is characterised among other things by a conceptual fluidity, a softening of boundaries, a quality which has often been called a unity of the arts. Architecture bleeds into sculpture, painting into scenography; forms are to be imagined washed in flickering lamplight, visual art to be enhanced by music. The artist merges with the artisan, the aesthete with the visionary, the intellectual with the sen-sualist. Artistic metaphor folds into the believer's willing suspension of disbelief. It's worth bearing in mind this elas-ticity when one tries to apply a clear-cut notion like 'author-ship' to St Peter's. All the artists who worked on the rebuilt church were in some sort of dialogue with each other, and with other buildings and earlier periods. The baldacchino is a prime example of this. It has been suggested that the design is not solely Bernini's at all (the execution certainly wasn't). Some commentators have claimed to see the hand of another artist in the baldacchino. Francesco Borromini was a rough contemporary of Bernini's, and, if the sources are right, his bitter rival. Lacking Bernini's polish and, cru-cially, his door-opening Florentine background – though as a native of what is now the Italian-speaking part of Switzerland he was a countryman, and indeed a relative, of Maderno and Fontana – Borromini was engaged in an artisanal capacity at St Peter's through the late 1610s and 1620s. He made a wrought-iron gate for the Chapel of the Sacrament, carved some stone cherubs in the entrance loggia and certainly worked on the baldacchino. The four marble pedestals supporting the structure are decorated with four extraordinary cartouches, richly ornamented elliptical frames. They are attributed in early accounts to a Francesco Fiammingo, which either misstates Borromini's origins or refers to yet another sculptor then working at St Peter's, Francois Duquesnoy (whom we would today call a Walloon rather than a Fleming). The cartouches show a woman's face in different stages of grimacing labour, with a smiling baby appearing at the last. The ovals surrounding each face bulge progressively further out from the plane of the surrounding

10. The baldacchino, by Bernini (and others?), 1624–33. The animated figures and the virtuoso treatment of small details like the tassels on the canopy make the structure occupy a strange hinterland between architecture and sculpture.

marble, and trail down into suggestively frilled and pleated ornament below. Explanations for this have ranged from a churlish reference to Bernini's mistress by his grudgeful rival, to a celebration of the delivery of a child to the Pope's niece, to an allegorical representation of the Church and St Peter's maternal status amongst churches.

Whoever executed the carving of the pedestals, there's no reason to say definitively that they weren't designed by Bernini, and it certainly can't be proved that Borromini or anyone else had any particular degree of involvement in the planning, as opposed to the making, of the baldacchino. Neither Borromini nor his early biographers give him credit. It's true that there is not much evidence for Borromini's involvement in the project at a creative level; but he did make several bold, free sketches of the baldacchino, which would have been useless as craftsman's working drawings, but seem to show an artist's sense of creative engagement. And the double curve of the 'Gothic' canopy is a motif which Borromini used in his later architectural career, on his minuscule if astonishingly inventive church of San Carlo alle Quattro Fontane up on the Quirinal hill and in the extensive facelift he gave to St John Lateran in preparation for the 1650 Jubilee, but which Bernini didn't. Contemporary biographical sources make the notion of any collaboration between Bernini and Borromini seem hard to credit; yet St Peter's is nothing if not a collaborative enterprise. The seventeenth century is when the church coalesces into a sort of unity in which ancient forms and contemporary preoccupations reach a workable compromise. It would be nice to think that the baldacchino, the spatial and iconographic linchpin of the entire building, was similarly collective in its conception as well as its execution.

Whatever the baldacchino is, and whatever it is for, and whoever designed and made it, it is by pacing around it that the visitor may at last begin to feel he or she has begun to get the measure of St Peter's for the first time. The eight ancient Solomonic columns transplanted into the crossing piers enter into a dialogue with their four bronze counterparts in the baldacchino. From the east, the baldacchino forms a picture-frame for the later Cathedra, distancing and disembodying it (we know Bernini foresaw this effect, as there's a delightfully squiggly drawing in the Vatican archives which shows the two structures interlocked, like the two sights on a sniper's rifle). One is still made to feel small. Since the eighteenth century it has been traditional to point out that Borromini's San Carlo alle Quattro Fontane – San Carlino is its nickname – could be made to fit entirely in one of the corner piers like the victim of a gangland slaying immured in some 60s flyover. The statues set into the piers, carved by Bernini and others, of St Longinus, St Veronica, St Helena and St Andrew, are around 4.5 metres high, more than twice life size. The double function of the church becomes clear: on the one hand, an abstract, meditative space, a monument to invisible ideas about memory, sacrifice and power, peopled with emblematic representations of hidden relics and deceased pontiffs, and on the other a useful one capable of moving thousands of visitors through itself like a heart pumping blood, of separating and addressing divergent and even incompatible sets of cultural and spiritual needs, and on occasion of uniting a vast crowd in contemplation of a single ritual or holding it in thrall to a single presence.

It is also from this point that a clear sense of the decorative unity imposed by Bernini on St Peter's may be had. In preparation for the Jubilee of 1650, under the Pamphili Pope Innocent X (famously painted by Velasquez, and less famously sculpted by Bernini), the church's interior was enriched. They faced the bare travertine arcades flanking the nave with coloured marbles, and inserted busts of early Popes, allegorical figures of various virtues and statues representing the founders of the religious orders which had proved so instrumental in the Catholic Church's riposte to Protestantism: quasi-military outfits like the Jesuits, and more fashionable organisations which served as a valuable conduit for funds from the wealthy and devout. After his death work carried on to Bernini's designs; new statues and facings were still being added during the twentieth century. The result is less ornate than it might appear in a smaller space (and much less so than many seventeenth- and eighteenth-century churches in certain parts of the Catholic world, such as Bohemia, Naples and Turin). Henry James wrote that St Peter's had a 'general beauty'. Even if most of the sculptures were 'either bad or indifferent; and the universal incrustation of marble, though sumptuous enough, has a less brilliant effect than much later work of the same sort', the overall effect was one of 'splendidly sustained simplicity'. But Bernini's interventions give lustre and movement to what might otherwise seem plodding and repetitive. Michelangelo is said to have wanted bare stone surfaces for his interior, but after Maderno's nave was added such a minimalist approach was probably felt to be too much of a good thing. Yet you don't have to be a Calvinist to find Bernini's decor oddly voluptuous for a place of worship. In the wake of the Counter-Reformation there are no problematic nudes or overt references to paganism. We have seen that under Bernini's chisel even martyrdom could be a subject packed with jollity. The longstanding notion that St Peter's was the Augustinian City of God, an idealised microcosm of the entire Christian community, demanded that it be peopled with the godly; while the biblical metaphor of the Church as the bride of Christ dictated that the bride look her best. But St Peter's displays a uniquely Baroque preoccupation with making a direct appeal to the senses. Its rich and varied colour doesn't come from the pictures, most of which are dwarfed by the space, but from the surfaces of the building itself: Carrara marble, snowdrift-white; red Sicilian jasper; the warm ochres of giallo antico; the mottled reds, blacks and whites of pavonazzetto; lamp-black schist from Belgium. Even without its population of ancient notables and Cardinal Virtues, the church would still provide plenty of occupation for the eye.

Marble is carnal stuff. Often it looks less like stone than food. Melted and churned by intense volcanic heat, its translucent, veined structure suggests pictorial decoration, or a brush swirled in water. The ancient Romans fell for it gradually, a process recorded with some distress by Pliny the Elder, for whom marble-mania was the 'foremost madness among our customs'. Trajan and Hadrian dressed their great public works in a many-coloured coat; a few scraps of pavonazzetto and giallo antico can still be seen in Trajan's forum, while the Pantheon retains a large part of its original decoration, a simple, multicoloured arrangement of different marbles known to the Romans as *opus sectile*, 'cut-up work'. Trajan's predecessor Domitian patronised a poet called Statius, who praised the wealth and taste of the Roman elite in a series of so-called 'villa poems'. Statius's poetry depicts a significant tension in Roman attitudes to luxury. His frank enjoyment of rich materials and elaborate spaces contrasts strongly with Pliny's soldierly asceticism of just some thirty years before. The great heroes of the Roman Republic had been men of abstemious habits such as Manius Curius, who said that nobody who was content to eat a supper of boiled turnips, as he was just preparing to do when visited by a party of Samnite ambassadors bearing gifts, ought to have any need of gold. But after a century of Empire, with the maternal embrace of the Pax Romana in full effect, people clearly grew more relaxed about leaving the soldiering to the professionals and enjoying some serious luxury. Statius's villa poems enumerate the precious materials, expert artistry and mod cons to be found in his patrons' houses as if he were a bailiff or an auctioneer. His collection is called *Silvae*, 'sticks', a word used to describe a rough draft, and there's a sense that he wants us to read these lists of things as fresh bundles of unprocessed, unmediated images and thoughts – though mediated and processed they assuredly are. Statius praises his patrons through their wealth and taste, but the relationship between the former and the latter is a tricky one for the modern reader to assess. 'Nothing plebeian there,' he says at one point, but in general you can't really tell from his treatment of their homes which of his patrons is a freedman and which the scion of a distinguished Republican family.

Here is a loose translation taken from an encomium he wrote about a villa on the end of the Sorrentine Peninsula south of Naples (a ruined maritime villa still exists near the apparent site). The artists Statius lists near the start are long-dead Greeks – Old Masters, if you like:

What's to say of ancient wax and bronze?
The colours of Apelles, Phidias's touch –
The blades of Polyclitus and of Myron.
Finer than gold the seized Corinthian bronze.

...

Here are rocks sliced out from Grecian caves,
Veined with sunlight from Syene's dawn,
Cut by Phrygian axes from sad fields,
Dappled with Cybele's doleful tears,
Etched with purple discs against the white.
Here's grass-green stone brought down from Mount
Taygetus;
Here yellow-glowing rocks from far Numidia;
From Thasos, and from Chios, and Carystos
Rippled like the waves, and full of joy.

You can see that Statius has a special soft spot for marble. The language he uses to describe it is breathily metaphorical. Veins are *picturata*, 'illustrated'. Pavonazzetto or Phrygian marble is stained with the blood of the lovesick king Attis, driven to self-mutilation by a mad desire for his grandmother, the goddess Cybele, the Great Mother (coincidentally worshipped on the Vatican hill, which in fact takes its name from her priests or *vates*), and by her remorseful tears. Stones invoke and embody the place they're from, and are often described with that place-name: Syene for red Aswan granite (strictly speaking, not a marble), Thasos for a white dolomitic rock quarried there, Chios for a greyish-white marble called portasanta in Italian, and so on. This emphasis on the far-flung origins of the different stones may imply that Statius saw marble as a fruit of Empire; in other words, Pliny was wrong, and *luxuria* of the sort displayed by Statius's patrons did not so much dissipate the Romans' manly bellicosity as feed off and celebrate it. That line about Corinthian bronze above suggests a similar belief; the metal was seen as precious by the Romans because it came from a sacked and subjugated city (it's just possible that Urban VIII thought something similar about the Pantheon – certainly there are plenty of references elsewhere to the re-use of antique materials being some sort of ritualised demonstration of the triumph of Christianity over paganism).

The marble decoration at St Peter's not only recalls antique prototypes, but also casts a new light on the Roman luxury debate. The use of different coloured marbles or *marmi mischi*, pioneered by Bernini in the Cornaro family chapel at Santa Maria della Vittoria in Rome, then applied more extensively at St Peter's and in many, many other churches during the later seventeenth and early eighteenth centuries, could be said to follow antique precedent, or even to demonstrate the surpassing of the ancients by the moderns. The Roman technique of *opus sectile* created lively decorative effects, but tended to be based on simple patterns of circles (often spare slices cut from columns, as – presumably – in the case of the St Peter's *rota*), squares, diamonds and so on. Seventeenth-century schemes tended to be significantly more elaborate and highly worked. Meanwhile, the blatant costliness and visual extravagance of *marmi mischi* might easily have been thought to undermine Christian virtues, just as Pliny had thought it undermined republican Roman ones. In the early sixteenth century, Michelangelo had defended his decision not to gild the ceiling of the Sistine Chapel by saying that the people he was depicting had been poor in life. More recently,

Caravaggio had won both praise and censure for the grubby realism of his biblical narratives; while the issue of luxury in church decoration was yet another quibble the Protestants had with Catholicism. Such decoration was enthusiastically embraced by the seventeenth-century Catholic Church. Probably this was a consequence of several different factors. First, it was in part a pragmatic policy designed to distinguish the True Faith as sharply as possible from drab, iconoclastic Protestantism. Second, it was clearly the wish of many Catholic organisations that their churches should resemble some sort of mystical revelation of Paradise. Third, Counter-Reformation Catholicism had unwritten the cool abstraction of much Renaissance theology and reverted to an almost medieval emphasis on direct, empathetic physical and emotional aspects of worship: transubstantiation, ecstasy, martyrdom. The coloured marbles encrusting the nave of St Peter's form a suitably sensual backdrop to the animated statues set into the nave walls, and the visceral experiences undergone by the saints depicted in the basilica's many altarpieces. Its gleaming marble surfaces of mottled reds and fatty whites give parts of the interior a weirdly anatomical character, as if the visitor were Jonah, cast into the belly of a giant fish – or, to allow a fanciful and impious thought to flit past us for a second, as if the identification of the Latin-cross church plan with the body of the crucified Christ were somehow closer than we thought, and our passage through the interior some strange inversion of the Eucharistic ritual.

So the crossing area of St Peter's affords some wide perspectives on the substance and meaning of the basilica, some more heterodoxical than others. It's a good place to begin to think about some powerful dialogues entered into by the building: between Renaissance and Baroque aesthetics, Neoplatonic and Counter-Reformation Catholicism, antiquity and modernity, architecture and the body, mass and space, structure and surface. As elsewhere, the 'imperfections' are as revelatory as anything. From the side you notice that Bernini's baldacchino is a few feet to the west of the centre of the crossing, and so doesn't sit as neatly as it might under the void created by the dome. From the nave, access to the baldacchino is anyway blocked by an elaborate sort of subway entrance, a D-shaped recess in the floor of the basilica with two curving flights of stairs – barricaded off from the public – and a dimly glittering shrine. This is the *confessio*, like the baldacchino which stands over it an important spatial and chronological marker. It gives access to the Grottoes, the extensive crypt underneath the nave and crossing. As of the middle of last century, it has also allowed entry to the Roman necropolis beneath that.

The *confessio* has two other functions. There are various references to Popes using it for private prayer, an opportunity to commune with the spirit of the papacy's first incumbent at important moments (see Chapter 1). Tucked into a little vaulted recess there is also a Byzantine icon of Christ, probably from the ninth century, one of very few examples of pre-Renaissance art visible from the main part of the basilica, even if you have to squint a bit to see it from above the *confessio*. This recess is called the niche of the pallium, palliums or pallia; it is from here that the woollen cloaks or scarves, decorated with silk crosses, are retrieved every 29 June and distributed by the Pope to the year's new crop of metropolitan bishops (as Bishop of Rome, any incoming Pope gets one too). The wool comes from two spring lambs blessed six months before in another Constantinian church, or rather a seventh-century church built by the ruins of a Constantinian one, Sant'Agnese fuori le Mura on Via Nomentana to the east of the city. St Agnes is associated with the Passion of Christ through the metaphor of the lamb, *agnus* in Latin. A mosaic of the Lamb of God flanked by Peter and Paul decorated the apse of Old St Peter's. In the eighteenth century, Pope Benedict XIV commissioned a silver urn to accommodate the palliums; before then, they used just to be dangled through the floor of the niche, into an unknown but sacred space below.

The fact that the pallium niche has been spared the rolling programme of 'improvements' applied elsewhere at St Peter's is an eloquent testimony to its significance, and to the antiquity of the rituals associated with it. More or less uniquely in a building dominated by different strains of architectural classicism, the niche is also pointedly off-centre. To find out why, you have to go and look beneath it.

5

THE SHRINE

*You have filled the whole world with tombs and sepulchres, and
yet in your Scriptures it is nowhere said that you must grovel
among tombs and pay them honour.*

Julian the Apostate, *Against the Galileans*

Visiting St Peter's in the mid-nineteenth century, Florence
Nightingale wrote that 'No event in my life except my death
can ever be greater than that first entrance into St Peter's, the
concentrated spirit of the Christianity of so many years, the
great image of our faith which is the worship of grief.' It's not
a perception of Catholicism which has much currency any
more, and possibly not one which the Church would nowadays much wish to promote. Good Friday is still a dolorous
affair in many towns across the Catholic world, with proces-
sions of cowled and, occasionally, self-flagellating *penitenti*
inching along from church to church; and many churches,
particularly in Spain's sphere of influence, contain gruesomely
lifelike images of tortured Christs and mutilated martyrs. But
the last Pope had a particular devotion to the Virgin Mary, a
more nurturing and pacific figure. Certainly St Peter's has its
share of horrors, though the size of the church makes them
less conspicuous than elsewhere. The layperson exploring the
church will recognise that many of the sculptures lining its

walls are monuments to the dead, but might never realise that the entire structure is built around a tomb.

The importance of the *confessio* in front of the papal altar is spatial – it gives access downwards, just where the dome wells upwards – and temporal, in that it is a place from which the oldest part of the church comes into contact with the new. The two curves of steps leading down are closed to the public. Access to the large crypt below the basilica, the area known as the Grottoes, is currently through an entrance on the north side of the basilica. The Grottoes are usually crowded with people who want to see, or rather photograph, the tomb of the last Pope. The consequent crush is regrettable, because there is some interesting stuff down there: fragments of antique masonry and ancient papal tombs from the old basilica, some odd bits of funerary sculpture from the nineteenth century and, in one chapel, an untypical and not entirely unsuccessful experiment in modernism. As for John Paul, his tomb reflects his simple habits: a plain marble plaque inscribed with his name, dates and *stemma* (a cross with an M for Mary in one corner), a glowing red lamp and – in a homely but rather surreal touch – two rubber plants.

In order to see the reverse angle of the view down from the nave into the *confessio* and the pallium niche, you have to join a guided tour round the Roman necropolis below the Grottoes. (Another necropolis has just opened to the public, beneath the car park near the basilica.) To do so you have to book, currently around a month in advance (see Planning a Visit?, page 215). Small groups are led round the bowels of the building on an enthralling but claustrophobia-inducing tour lasting around an hour and a half. The English-speaking guides are usually sleek seminarians. The character of the 'Scavi tour' is emphatically religious rather than art-historical or archaeological, though the guides seem to know what they're talking about. When I took it we finished with a prayer.

Down a narrow flight of stairs from the southern side of the Grottoes, through a *Star Trek*-style airlock, up a few steps and round a corner is the most dramatic part of the Vatican necropolis, the 'street of tombs'. This is immediately recognisable as a suburban Roman necropolis of a kind you can see at Pompeii or Ostia. It is sometimes identified as the Via Cornelia, which sources say ran parallel to the north side of Nero's circus. As much as anything it resembles a row of houses, faced in brick, stucco and *opus reticulatum*, a characteristic Roman technique of pyramidal stones pushed into a mortar base to make a diamond- or literally net-shaped pattern, with marble *cippi* or inscribed tablets over the doors and set into the walls. It is an extraordinary thing to find under such a vast building, even if it is only along a portion of the 'street' that the tombs can really be seen in anything like their original state. Later additions, the foundations of Constantine's basilica, the *muro divisorio* built by Antonio da Sangallo to close off its eastern stump in the sixteenth century and the footings of Bernini's bronze baldacchino have all obliterated portions of the earlier structures. The jumble of tombs and sarcophagi in certain areas has made full excavation impossible. But the necropolis is still a remarkable survival: all the more so because of a complex of buildings at the western edge of the excavated area.

When Pope Pius XII and Ludwig Kaas, the administrator of the Fabbrica, began excavations under the Vatican Grottoes in 1939, the position of Peter's tomb had always been agreed, but never in any way substantiated. In the fourth century CE, when Constantine and his successors embarked on their church-building bonanza, the architects of St Peter's clearly thought they knew where it was. Successive elaborations and rebuildings, whether planned or executed, continued to mark the same spot, either in the centre of the semicircular apse at the western end of the old church, or near the centre of the crossing of the new one. But there was no systematic exploration of what might lie beneath – understandably, given the delicate issue of tomb displacement which the rebuilding programme had already provoked. A workman had fallen into a tomb in 1574, and sketched a glittering mosaic he found there. A few discoveries had been made since, including several burials brought to light when Bernini's workmen were laying the foundations for the baldacchino in the 1620s. In the nineteenth century a Jesuit lowered a light fifteen feet into a hole in the bottom of the pallium niche – though he couldn't see anything. But works begun under Pope Pius XI, predecessor to Pius XII, to lower the floor of the Grottoes had revealed the four walls of a substantial second-century tomb: a richly-articulated room, with niches for cinerary urns set into the walls, and enchanting wall-decorations in fresco and stucco. Although most of the iconography in the tomb was pagan, a girl called Emilia Gorgonia was commemorated with what looked like Christian imagery: doves, a woman drawing water from a well and the Latin phrase 'dormit in pace', 'she sleeps in peace'. The coexistence of different belief-systems in a single Roman necropolis was not unusual, but given Christianity's equivocal status at the time, and given that this was a single vault dedicated to one *familia*, a term which might encompass slaves and freedmen as well as blood relations, but which ordinarily would tend to denote some degree of intimacy, this was an intriguing find.

Pius XI was not inclined to follow it up, but his successor lost no time in setting up an excavation. Certain rules would apply. Any human remains discovered were to be brought to Monsignor Kaas for blessing and safe keeping. Digging was not to take place in the extra-sensitive area under the crossing. To preserve the secrecy of the project, all work was to be done while the basilica was closed, and all the spoil from the dig was to be disguised as part of a landscaping project in the Vatican gardens. Through the dismal war years and afterwards, the excavations continued in strict silence. More and more instances of Christian burials cheek-by-jowl with pagan cremations were unearthed (though burial was not automatically a sign of Christianity, nor cremation of paganism; inhumation was the preferred option in the Eastern half of the Roman world, where people were more influenced by Egyptian and Semitic practices). Several *cippi* had been flipped over and their backs engraved with Christian messages rather than pagan ones, cruder in execution and probably later in date.

This was a puzzle. The building of St Peter's in, let's say, the 320s and 330s CE obviously rendered the pagan tombs inaccessible (it also destroyed several of them completely, since the flat floor level of the basilica necessitated gouging into the higher ground to the north-west just as it did building a terrace on massive foundations to the lower south-east; even in the 'street of tombs' the roofs and upper storeys have been sliced off). So either the Christians had already started to be buried alongside their pagan contemporaries before the Edict of Milan, in which case attitudes to Christianity may have been softer than standard accounts of the faith's early years suggest; or they slotted themselves into existing tombs in a fairly short time, after the Edict of Milan but before the building of the basilica. One possible scenario is some sort of formal amnesty whereby pagans, who wouldn't like their ancestors to be buried under thousands of tons of basilica where they couldn't drop by once in a while and leave them offerings, may have been given some opportunity to get out, while Christians, who didn't need such close physical access to their dead but would be delighted to think of them being interred so close to a certified apostle, moved in. This is the hypothesis advanced by the Vatican guides. Certainly, much of the Christian imagery in the necropolis is accepted to be Constantinian (the numerous Chi-Rho motifs found on the site, for example, are unlikely to be earlier, as the sign is associated with the eve of the Battle of Milvian Bridge – see Chapter 2). But a few inscriptions appear to be earlier, and it is these that aroused the greatest excitement during the excavations and subsequently.

After a couple of years the Pope gave permission for the excavators to start digging in the holiest area of the necropolis, the area under the papal altar and the baldacchino. Here they found that the concentration of Christian burials – and Christian graffiti – increased. Here also was the tomb disturbed by accident in the sixteenth century, with a lovely mosaic of Helios or Sol the sun-god, an avatar of Apollo, but also of Christ. Constantine certainly identified Christ pretty closely with Helios (see Chapter 2), though the anecdote that he erected a statue of himself as Helios in Byzantium with the nails from the True Cross radiating from its head to form the sun-god's characteristic Statue of Liberty nimbus is sadly unreliable, if widely quoted in Byzantine sources. Less well preserved is another mosaic, representing a fisherman, a common metaphor for Christ's mission, and, of course, Peter's first profession. A third depicts Jonah and the whale ('giant fish' is what the Bible actually says), an interesting choice both because Jonah was the name of Peter's father, and because his temporary sojourn in the slippery darkness is a widely used Christian allegory of death and resurrection (the charioteer has a similar meaning of course, bringing back day after night).

As the interest and implications of the necropolis grow greater, so its physical appearance gets more and more confusing. The problem is a common one with archaeological sites, where there is either too little material left to give you a clear idea what once went on, or too much from too many different periods. Strict environmental controls are also in operation in the Vatican necropolis, so many tombs are glazed in and can't be seen as clearly as one might wish – though a systematic programme of restoration and lighting redesign does ensure everything looks its best, in a slightly stagey way. But if you take the tour, a sense of mounting excitement is hard to ignore. The excavations offer a strange repetition of the architectural arrangement above: the street of tombs echoing the linearity of the nave, the gathering feeling of density and meaning and the sense of encircling something of profound ritual importance as you reach the central area. The fact that one occasionally encounters evidence of the present and previous structures above – the semicircular form of Constantine's apse, the sarcophagi let down into the floor of the ancient basilica and now perched at headheight in the semi-excavated portion of the necropolis, the great foundation walls (the buried tombs effectively formed part of the foundations as well), the massive blocks supporting Bernini's baldacchino, the grilles let into the floor of the Grottoes by Pius XII when he replaced the floor with reinforced concrete in 1948 – makes one feel as if one is exploring the engine-room of a great battleship. The necropolis not only constitutes a curious mirror-image of the physical fabric of St Peter's, but also, little by little, reveals the secret of its unique spiritual authority. That such a revelation might also be a demystification – proof denies faith, after all – seems not to have troubled the authorities, although it may be one reason why the necropolis is not easier to visit.

The area under the baldacchino is not easy to describe, so here's a simplified reconstruction (Fig. 11). The natural incline running diagonally uphill from south-west to north-east is revealed in a short flight of steps. Near this is what's left of a short wall (A), running from south to north, rendered and painted in a simple coating of red ochre. A pair of columns bridged by an entablature and set in front of this so-called 'red wall' frames a partly preserved rectangular grave covered with a pitched terracotta canopy (B). The upper part hasn't survived, but is usually reconstructed as I've shown it with a triangular pediment (on the basis of broadly similar structures elsewhere). Just to the north of the tabernacle is another wall (C), embedded into the red wall and sticking out at right angles to it. This is called the 'graffiti wall' on account of the multitude of inscriptions scratched into it. It was initially thought to be either a buttress, propped up against the red wall at some wobbling phase of its early history, or a sort of embankment stabilising a higher ground level to the north. Several graves were scattered near this structure, though

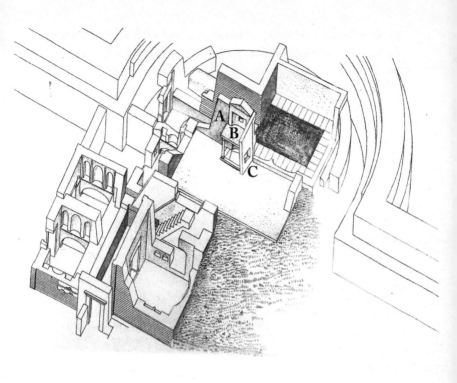

11. Axonometric view (sketch reconstruction) of the red wall area beneath St Peter's. I've exaggerated the niche in the graffiti wall (C) where the bones said to be Peter's were found. The curved wall framing the structures is the foundations of Constantine's apse. Behind the red wall area is a courtyard and a small enclosure which contained Christian tombs, and which has been called the world's first cathedral. The tombs in the lower part of the image are mostly pagan; the doorway at bottom left leads to the so-called 'street of tombs'.

most of them are no longer visible. Those closest to the grave under the red wall tended to be parallel with it, misaligned by around 11° from the wall and the prevailing east–west orientation of the street.

When the area round the red wall was unearthed, it was immediately clear that this was the tomb believed in the basilica's early history to be Peter's, the so-called Tropaion or 'trophy' mentioned by Gaius, the secretary of Pope Zephirinus, at the turn of the third century in a letter quoted by Eusebius over a century later. Gaius's choice of words has been much pored over. A trophy implies a military monument, traditionally an enemy's armour piled up to suggest a turning point – the etymological source of the word 'trophy' is *trephō*, 'turn' – in a battle. Related imagery was co-opted in the Renaissance to suggest the Christian's conquest of death. A trophy is also not quite the same thing as a tomb, and so doesn't need a body; just because it was put up to honour Peter on the Vatican hill doesn't mean he had actually to be buried there. The identification of the tomb with Gaius's was not so much because of the tomb's layout or appearance, which were not particularly distinctive, nor because of the graffiti, which would yet take some time to decipher. The relative importance of the area was clear from the scrum of burials nearby. The fact that some of them lay parallel with that under the Tropaion – that is, out of kilter with the prevailing layout elsewhere in the necropolis – suggests that these burials predated the building of the more elaborate architectural tombs, most of which seem to date from the second century CE or later. Most significantly, the red wall lay beneath and within three later layers – four if you count Clement VIII's altar above. A marble and porphyry rectangle enclosing the tomb seemed to be the *memoria*, the shrine erected round the tomb at the basilica's inception (d). This can be seen on the Pola casket mentioned in Chapter 4; it is nowadays visible from the back through a grille set above the altar of Clement VIII's chapel in the Grottoes – the place from which the excavators burrowed in. Above and around the *memoria*, Pope Gregory I, the Great, set an altar when he remodelled the western end of the basilica around the turn of the seventh century. This was wrapped in yet another layer by Callixtus II in the twelfth century. This altar determined the position of Clement's altar above it, but was otherwise buried during the rebuilding of St Peter's. But the *confessio*, the processional stairway down to the level of the Grottoes and the pallium niche, can be seen as an elaboration of the arrangement introduced under Gregory when he raised the floor level of the apse and created a crypt beneath it. Similar arrangements exist at San Paolo fuori le Mura – remember the traditional symmetry between Peter and Paul – and at St John Lateran, where the baldacchino frames a ciborium, a grandiose multiple reliquary containing fragments of bone harvested from all twelve apostles.

Before we start to try to work out whether Peter really was buried by the red wall in the Vatican necropolis, we ought to weigh up the early Christians' reasons for believing that he was. The ancient but unreliable *Liber Pontificalis* says that Peter's successor-but-one Anacletus erected a tomb to the apostle, and that the early leaders of the church were buried next to him. This may be a mistaken reference to Anicetus, who held the pontificate in the mid-second century, which would be about right for the apparent date of the Tropaion (and would suggest that the burial and the tomb were not contemporary, thereby accounting for the 11° misalignment). The *Liber Pontificalis* also says that Constantine dressed and honoured Peter's body, and that he and his mother Helena, by all accounts a rather more devout Christian than her son, put an inscribed gold cross into his tomb (this was allegedly glimpsed by Giacomo della Porta when falling masonry cracked the floor of the church in 1594. It was shown to Clement VIII, then piously sealed up again). But Constantine may have brought the body from elsewhere, for example San Sebastiano on the Appian Way, which in the years before the Edict of Milan accommodated the earthly remains of many Christian martyrs. More compelling in a way is Gaius's comment that you can see the tombs of the founders of Christianity in the Vatican and on the Via Ostiense, a clear reference to Peter and Paul, even if it might also encompass whomever else was then deemed important enough to be a 'founder'. The *Acts of St Peter*, a rather dubious third-century text (the one which says the apostle was martyred in the Naumachia near Nero's obelisk on the mountain, see Chapter 2), claims that the body was hidden in the tomb of a fellow-Christian, a senator called Marcellus – but doesn't say how the Christians got hold of the body, or where this ad hoc entombment took place.

Peter's status as an executed criminal is crucial. Ordinarily such bodies – and there were plenty – were left to rot, thrown into the Tiber, or maybe burned unceremoniously. One might think that anybody building monuments to such a non-person would be unlikely to escape some sort of persecution in turn. It is hard to reconcile the insistence of early Christian sources on Rome's implacable hostility towards their religion with the same sources' implication that famous tombs were already an object of a kind of pilgrimage a century and a half before the Edict of Milan. One way round the problem, the catacomb, is plainly irrelevant in the case of the Vatican necropolis, which wasn't underground then, although it looks as though it is now, and which retained a healthy proportion of pagan tombs right up to the time of Constantine. But a kind of *samizdat* worship, conducted within family tombs and walled compounds outwardly indistinguishable from conventional pagan memorials, is easy to imagine. Roman cemeteries were fairly busy places (widely used by unlicensed prostitutes, among other things), and devotees of one cult might not be too worried about what devotees of another were up to next door.

It is also important to bear in mind the difference between Christian and pagan attitudes to death and the dead. Not all Romans espoused the extreme materialism – or, if you prefer, the woolly pantheism – of the Stoics, for whom death was a reabsorption of the individual soul into the collective world-spirit, after which only inert and irrelevant matter remained: ashes to ashes, indeed. Christianity was just one belief-system among several which laid more and more stress on the survival of the individual consciousness after death. Devotees of Isis or Mithras might have a much clearer sense of an afterlife than followers of more traditional cults, for instance. But such beliefs were not especially widespread. The classical myth of Hades, wherein lay the slender possibility that a blissful stint in the Elysian Fields might be followed by a sip of the waters of forgetfulness and eventual reincarnation, must to most pagan Romans have seemed as fanciful as the Christian concepts of death, judgement, heaven and hell. Many must still at the time of Milan have thought that if we survive death it is not as ourselves, but as impersonal fragments of something larger. One pagan inscription from the Vatican necropolis, written by a father to his dead child, sums this view up with delicacy and grace: 'Here lies Optatus, a child noble in piety, whose ashes I pray become violets and roses: and that the earth who is now his mother lie light on him, for in life he lay heavy on nobody.' The inscription shows, among other things, that what might seem like a decidedly comfort-less metaphysics still allowed pagan Romans a rich and even tender relationship with their dead – something the bustling ritual life of the Roman necropolis would tend to affirm.

So let's say it's around 200 CE. The Christians of Rome meet in private houses, and bury their dead in secret (or possibly not so secret) caves and, here and there, slip them into existing pagan cemeteries. In everything they have to be cautious about revealing their identity, so as well as a private language of signs and symbols like the fish (the first letters of the Greek words for 'Jesus Christ, Son of God, Saviour' spell *ichthus*, the Greek word for a fish), they adapt the prevailing pagan iconography to symbolise their own needs, with Bacchic imagery evoking the Eucharist, Apollonian or heliolatrous imagery suggesting a cycle of death and resurrection, Isis and Harpocrates/Osiris standing in for Mary and Christ, and so on (this conflation of imagery may or may not represent some blending of belief, just as in a Roman client kingdom the local deities tended to blur into imported Graeco-Roman ones). Christian visitors to the Caput Mundi make sure to visit the graves of their illustrious predecessors, and maybe even undertake the journey especially in order to do so, an early example of Christian pilgrimage. In the Vatican necropolis, a simple tomb or tabernacle, nowhere explicitly identified as the tomb of St Peter, is nonetheless widely believed so to be. It stands in a little courtyard, with steps leading up to a corridor running behind giving access to two small rooms. Visitors scratch into the walls their prayers, names, signs of their faith and so on. Burials are made as close to the tomb as possible. Other rituals – Eucharist, marriage, ordination, who knows – are perhaps also conducted there, all under the noses of the pagans who continue to toast their gone-for-good loved ones with libations and sweet cakes just a few feet away. The scenario is at least feasible, though the pagans in question would have to be tolerant – or pretty incurious – for it to be really practical.

The question facing the archaeologists was whether the material evidence on the site bore out the version of events set out in the sources, and long ago incorporated into Vatican folklore. Constantine's cross couldn't really be expected to turn up after all this time, especially since a violent sack by the Saracens in 846 CE. But here was his *memoria*, and here was what looked very much like Gaius's Tropaion inside it. The momentum of the project gradually intensified. In 1949 the *New York Times* published a leaked story about the dig, complete with excited references to 'bones in an urn'. Several bones, not to mention several urns, had indeed been discovered by that point, both in the Early Christian part of the necropolis and elsewhere. Golden votives of some antiquity, possibly even Constantinian, were found near the red wall. In 1950, a Jubilee year, Pius publicly announced that his archaeologists had located Peter's tomb and were examining remains found there. Two hundred and fifty bones and bits of bone had been placed at the Pope's feet when he rushed down to the dig as soon as he heard that the archaeologists had begun to explore the foot of the red wall. But this promising midden proved a disappointment. The fact that nothing there looked like a skull was good news, as tradition held that Peter's head had been removed for safe keeping before the Saracens came, and indeed that it now resided in the ciborium at St John Lateran. But anthropologist Venerando Correnti of Palermo University patiently examined the bones from 1956 and found that they came from at least four different people, one of them a woman, and indeed that around a quarter of them were animal bones, which seems an odd way to honour an apostle. Later carbon-dating would also reveal that they weren't as old as they needed to be to vindicate any claim to apostolic pedigree.

Meanwhile an epigrapher, Margarita Guarducci, had arrived on site in 1952 and set to work trying to piece together the constellations of graffiti on the Tropaion and elsewhere. It was she who decided that a graffito in the tomb of Valerius Herma, a little way back to the east, included a reference to Peter, albeit not a very literate one: ... *hominibus Crestianus* [sic] *ad corpus tuum sepultis*, '[pray for] the Christian men buried near your body'. This was near a scratched image of a face, which she took to be Peter's, and another which she took to be Christ's (though it takes a certain level of imagination even to see the second face as a face). This lent a double fillip to the excavators. The reference to Peter was exciting enough; but the inscription also seemed to vindicate, or at least furnish an ancient precedent for, what had since the Reformation been the specifically Catholic notion of Purgatory. If you're in heaven there's no need for your loved ones to pray for you, and if you're in hell there's no point in them doing so. In her researches Guarducci found many Christian graffiti – alphas and omegas, chis and rhos, even, in what looked like a specifically Petrine variant, Chi-Rhos with extra Es added to make complex pictograms which punned on the Latin and Greek alphabets (a Greek rho looking like a Latin 'P') and perhaps even the visual motif of Peter's heavenly key (not otherwise known at this time so far as I'm aware). Among the rash of barely visible letters on the graffiti wall she identified a version of the angel's promise to Constantine: [in] ho[c] vin[ce], or, the sceptic might point out, 'ho vin', which could mean a number of things.

Then things took an unexpected turn. A *sampietrino* called Giovanni Segoni, who had worked on the dig from the outset, told Margarita Guarducci that some ten years before more remains had been found, not in the area below the red wall, but in a small cavity, lined with marble, in the graffiti wall. These had been removed by Monsignor Kaas without his briefing any of the archaeologists or documenting the removal in any way. They had also remarkably slipped his mind during the intervening period. Segoni led Guarducci to the storeroom and showed her a wooden box, on which he himself had written *ossa – urna – graf*, the bones from the urn (the marble compartment) in the graffiti wall. The bones were retrieved from storage and subjected to a careful examination. This time the auspices were more positive. These were the bones of a single elderly man, stocky in build. His feet were missing, which they might be if he'd been crucified upside down and hastily hacked free. He had a head, or part of one, which meant there might be a few questions to be asked about what was in the reliquary in St John Lateran. His remains had been wrapped in a purple cloth with gold embroidery.

The archaeologists' attention was brought forcibly back to

some of the other materials found in this cavity in the graffiti wall. Some medieval coins and enamel had been found, as well, crucially, as a fragment of the red wall inscribed with a Greek graffito thought to read *Petros eni*, an abbreviation of *Petros enesthi*, Peter is inside. Without the human remains little had been made of this before, but now it took on a new significance. In 1963, just after the accession of Paul VI, Guarducci told the incoming Pope (a family friend) that the bones were indeed Peter's. She said the same in a book published, to mixed response, in 1965. For the bones to be genuine they would have had to have been moved to this particularly furtive location at some point in the Tropaion's pre-Constantine history, as the Tropaion and the graffiti wall didn't exist when Peter was martyred. Stashing the bones in what looked like a perfectly innocuous piece of buttressing next to the 'official' grave might have been an elegant piece of reverse psychology, and was anyway easier than dragging them all the way down to San Sebastiano or wherever. The hypothesis restored an edge of danger to early Christian ritual, as it implied that there was something for the Christians of the Vatican necropolis to fear after all. It also explained one of the more puzzling features of the pallium niche as seen from the basilica above: its asymmetricality. If the builders of the first basilica understood the Tropaion to be a lopsided structure, that is, if the graffiti wall was understood to be an important part of the whole, then they would have centred their building on that whole, and the point of access into the area between the columns of the Tropaion and the 'official' grave beneath would have been a little to the left, or south, of centre, as it is. Otherwise even the dwindling architectural sensibilities of the fourth century would have demanded that the 'tabernacle' – the pair of columns set in front of the red wall – formed the lodestone of the whole basilica.

Many questions were still left unanswered. The original archaeological team was criticised for careless documentation of their work (for example, the accusation was made that a tent-shaped ridge in the foundations of the red wall was initially documented as an accidental flaw rather than evidence that the wall was built to fit carefully over an existing grave). Guarducci and others, notably Engelbert Kirschbaum, a Jesuit who had been involved in the excavations at every stage, rebutted their critics vigorously. But a completely plausible historical narrative was still elusive. If the bones had once been in the grave under the red wall, who had moved them? The marble box in the graffiti wall was generally supposed to be Constantinian, so why didn't he just move the bones back into the space between the columns of the Tropaion? With a great big basilica built around them they would hardly be at the mercy of the elements any more, and the need for concealment ought in theory to have evaporated. The functional importance of the remains would primarily have been their role in the creation of what are called 'contact relics' – objects which are sanctified by being placed next to a saint's remains (a pallium is a modern example of a contact relic). Yet the marble repository is set into the north side of the graffiti wall – that is, the opposite side to the space below the pallium niche. Constantine's *memoria* rendered it entirely inaccessible. It's hard to avoid the conclusion that the builders of Old St Peter's thought the apostle's remains lay below the red wall, and that the graffiti wall was an integral, but not entirely essential, part of the arrangement. In which case either the repository is pre-Constantinian, or it was thought to contain someone reasonably important, maybe even an early Pope, but not Peter himself.

Whether you believe that the fragmentary structure now forming the climax of the Scavi tour beneath St Peter's really is Peter's tomb, and whether you believe that the bones said to have been so reverently tucked in such an unprepossessing location in the graffiti wall really are Peter's earthly remains, is really a question of faith. Meaning not only religious faith, but also faith in the integrity and objectivity of the individuals concerned. Some of the evidence seems compelling, though nothing perhaps is so compelling as the simple fact that such a difficult site was chosen for such an ambitious construction purely in order that the basilica have the Tropaion at its heart. Many of the graffiti are incontestably to do with Peter. But the chain of evidence, as they would say in a police-procedural drama, is broken. The Vatican has been a centre of outstanding scholarship for centuries, but it is also justly notorious for censorship, secrecy and the repression of scientific truth. It was an astonishing breach of protocol, to put it no higher, for Ludwig Kaas to take remains offsite and let them gather dust for so long. Some of the most suggestive graffiti are also the hardest to read. Nevertheless, the official story is that both tomb and remains are genuine. Pius's successor Paul VI allowed the bones from both red and graffiti walls to be carbon-dated – only the latter were found to be first-century – and ordered the head in the Lateran to be examined by Venerando Correnti, though he forbade the publication of any detailed findings. That turned out to have only skull fragments in it, too desiccated for particularly close analysis, so could have come from the body in the Vatican (which has very few skull bones left). Now the authorities were in no doubt. In June 1968, just a couple of days before St Peter and St Paul's day, the graffiti wall bones were pronounced by Paul to be genuine. The following day they were reinserted into the graffiti wall, entombed anew in a stack of high-tech plastic boxes donated to the Holy See by NASA, in plenty of time for that year's palliums to be lowered into the rococo casket overhead. All the other human remains found in the Vatican necropolis, pagan and Christian alike, have been removed and reburied elsewhere.

What cannot be questioned is the importance of the Tropaion to the builders of the first basilica and their successors. Yet in its changes over time, the area around and over the tomb reflects its changing significance. Constantine's *memoria* was a reliquary, a ceremonial box with an arched entrance in the front, allowing cloths and votive offerings to be placed close to the Tropaion, either by pilgrims or clergy, and blessed (evidently the origin of the pallium ritual). It stood on the floor of the church; a perforated marble slab, the so-called 'Isidorus' slab, covered the pitched terracotta grave. Six twisted columns framed the arrangement and connected it with the walls of the apse. By the time of Gregory the Great, the nature of the Church, the papacy and the ritual life of the practising Christian had all evolved. The fabled simplicity of Early Christian habits had given way to something a little more grand. Papal bureaucracy had become more settled and more hierarchical. Swelling numbers meant that the Eucharist was something performed for a congregation rather than simply shared among a community (a shift in meaning which would culminate at the Council of Trent, still nearly a millennium in the future). Gregory's alterations reflect these changes. He raised the floor of the apse, the symbolic domain of the clergy, above that of the laity in the nave. Set into the curve of the apse itself was a curved seat for the elders, a synthronon or presbytery, and in the very centre of the apse wall, in a spot corresponding with that which in the rebuilt church would be occupied by Bernini's Cathedra, a bishop's throne. From this vantage point the Bishop – that is, the Pope – and his colleagues could perform Mass on the altar which now crowned the apostle's tomb. That was, if not demoted, then certainly made less prominent in the overall arrangement, even if an additional gift of five Solomonic columns in the eighth century allowed the new refinement of two impressive parallel screens of six across the mouth of the apse. Pilgrims now had to go beneath the raised apse area to see whatever they could still see of the *memoria*. The mosaic which today adorns the pallium niche is ninth-century – with some still later additions – but it may well indicate an earlier boxing-in of the Tropaion.

Gregory was a powerful political figure, who consolidated and increased the Popes' temporal power two centuries before Charlemagne. He bypassed the Byzantine exarchate at Rimini to treat with the Lombards directly, and expanded the papal estates around Rome. His vision of the Archangel Michael sheathing his fiery sword over the ruins of Hadrian's second-century mausoleum was believed to be a sign that a recent plague was ending, but it led to the mausoleum being transformed into the Castel Sant'Angelo, an emphatically martial presence on the Roman skyline and a potent assertion of potential independence. His decision to step into Constantine's shoes and remodel St Peter's should thus be seen at least partly as being an early sign of the papacy's growing desire to make a new dispensation with imperial power. Emphasising the priestly task of Mass at the business end of St Peter's, and making the apostle's tomb less conspicuous in the process, could be seen as a step in a similar direction. As important a figure as the apostle was, Peter's brand of Christianity predated the issue of Pope versus Emperor by nearly three centuries. His lesson was one of meekness and submission, and so not especially useful to a forward-looking pontiff. Later on, of course, in the Middle Ages, the Popes' main rivals were the baronial families of Rome, and the idea of the Petrine succession became more important again, demonstrating the longevity of papal claims on temporal power and asserting the Popes' independence of an often hostile Empire. This is one reason why the main papal seat was moved in the fifteenth century from the Lateran – conventionally held to have been a gift from Constantine – to the Vatican, site of Nero's most fabulous atrocities.

Touring the tombs under the basilica is not necessarily the best way to understand how they fit together, or how they fit in with the rest of the basilica. From below you can't really see the Isidorus slab, and you certainly can't see that there's a hole in it. And the Tropaion doesn't look much like its reconstructions, more like a random fudgelike mass of brick and masonry. But you do get to see some pretty Roman tomb decorations in marble, stucco, mosaic and paint. And at the end of the tour you see the bones in question, peeping from their cracked marble cradle, safe and inert in their untarnished Plexiglas sepulchres. It seems an odd way for an apostle – or anyone else – to end up.

6

A SCHOOL FOR ARTISTS

*The tomb of Alexander VII has eight or ten peasants from the
Sabine hills stalled in front of it with their mouths open ...
no doubt they return to their mountains better Catholics after
having seen the skeleton.*

Stendhal, *Promenades dans Rome*

In 1694 Carlo Fontana, then the basilica's architect, wrote
a history of St Peter's. His conclusion was nothing if not
laudatory: 'This Vatican Temple being so worthy, so eye-
catching, so magnificent as to terrify the most sublime intel-
lect with its very prospect ... to the shame of all ill-wishers
will live, and will last forever, growing greater, for the glory
of Our Faith, of Rome and of the whole Catholic World.'
He also expressed the hope that it be a 'school for artists', a
sentiment which had by then become commonplace. Many
famous artists have indeed worked there. Giotto, Filarete and
Pollaiuolo produced works for the old basilica which were
then transplanted into the new one, as did Michelangelo,
who carved his beautiful *Pietà* at the end of the fifteenth
century (Fig. 12). A hundred years later Caravaggio painted
an altarpiece which spent all of a week in situ before being
packed off elsewhere; the great Bolognese Baroque master
Guercino produced a huge altarpiece in 1623; five years later,

12. The *Pietà* by Michelangelo, 1498–9. The sculpture was restored and perhaps altered after being broken en route to its present location in the eighteenth century. It was also attacked with a hammer by one Laszlo Toth in 1972 (He shouted, 'I am Jesus Christ!' as he struck home). It's now behind bullet-proof glass.

the French emigré Nicholas Poussin got an early commission to paint a particularly unpleasant martyrdom; there are tombs by Bernini and Canova; and so on. Most of the art in the church dates from the period when New St Peter's was being built, the sixteenth and seventeenth centuries; but as well as a few survivors from earlier periods there are also a handful of more recent works from the eighteenth to the twentieth centuries. These, in truth, don't make much of an impact. But they do express the taste, and some of them at least the religious culture, of their times, just as Bernini gives emphatic expression to those of his.

Having said that, it is a hopelessly broad question to ask what the works of art lining the aisles and side-chapels of St Peter's are for. In large part they are meant to do what art does in Catholic churches everywhere: act as foci for religious worship, glorify the patrons of the church, document its history and so on. This, in the eyes of at least some visitors, is what they continue to do; others see them as works of art which happen to be in a church rather than a museum, objects which ought to be looked at in some sort of mental isolation, which document a belief-system and its political superstructure in much the same way as a collection of tribal artefacts might disclose the customs of a vanished, undeveloped people to a keen-eyed ethnographer, but which to the layperson might just as well be judged on aesthetic grounds alone.

Then there is the simple fact that individual works of art at St Peter's tend to be shouted down by the basilica's sheer size. Where a single tomb or altarpiece might dominate a smaller church, in St Peter's even the gigantic can seem lonely and inconsequential. There is also the problem of what might be called the patina of the building. The materials used in the tombs, whether Pollaiuolo and Manzù's bronze, Canova's white marble or Bernini's gaudy polychromy, echo and blend with the architectural forms surrounding and overarching them. It takes a certain effort to see even some of the most impressive as autonomous works of art rather than simply part of the furniture (much of the seventeenth-century sculptural decoration effectively is part of the furniture). Most of the paintings in the basilica anyway turn out on closer inspection not to be paintings at all. What purport to be original works by Guercino, Poussin or whomever are really copies made by the skilled artisans of the Vatican's in-house mosaic studio.

Since the late sixteenth century, when a team of Venetians decorated the Gregorian chapel in mosaic and the Roman Cavaliere d'Arpino designed figures of the Apostles and Evangelists to decorate the inside of the dome, the Fabbrica has pursued a policy of commissioning mosaic decorations for St Peter's, and later of rendering its existing paintings into mosaic. A specialist institution was set up for the purpose in the early eighteenth century. During the eighteenth and nineteenth centuries, mosaic became a favourite material for luxury diplomatic gifts. Alumni of the studio also went into private practice, and produced expensive souvenirs of the Eternal City for travellers. The techniques of the modern Roman mosaicists far outstripped those of their ancient compatriots. Yet a law of diminishing returns, familiar to anybody who has watched the development of painting and sculpture through the 'academic' centuries of the Western tradition, decrees that technical accomplishment is no guarantee of charm. The tesserae used by ancient mosaicists were little cuboid chips, either of coloured stone or pigmented glass, usually around six millimetres along a side and roughly finished. Some small figurative scenes were done with smaller pieces. But the exhilarating impression one gets from a good classical mosaic is that the often remarkable illusion of reality one sees has been achieved somewhat against the odds. Increasingly, of course, in later antiquity and still more in Byzantine art, illusionism became less of a priority, and other things – the mineral lustre of the materials, the tiny variations in placement creating additional lighting effects, the very intimacy (or spiritual intensity) which such a naïve representational style can invite – came to the fore. The kindest commentator on the St Peter's mosaics would have to concede that intimacy is not something they invite in large measure. As for spiritual intensity – well, that depends on the spirit concerned, I suppose.

Nevertheless, it is an achievement of a sort to have made a series of such precise copies of so many important Renaissance and Baroque paintings. The Vatican mosaicists used their extraordinarily laborious technique to match the tiniest details of paintings like Guercino's *St Ludmilla* or Raphael's *Transfiguration* (a painting which never hung in St Peter's but which has been scaled up in mosaic and now forms one of the most prominent elements of its pictorial decoration): more remarkably, they also managed to imitate the colour effects employed by different artists – the airy Venetian palette of the early Poussin, the stormy blues and warm earth colours of Domenichino and Guercino, the hard bright colours of Raphael. Since the original oil paintings on which the St Peter's mosaics are based arrive at their colour effects laboriously, by means of layering, glazing and scumbling, this is quite something in a medium in which the only mixture of colours possible must be made to take place in the eye.

Still, the mosaics are documents of absent originals. Some of their parents can be seen up the hill in the Vatican museums; others are farther afield. Giotto's *Navicella*, an image of Christ calming the stormy Sea of Galilee, and urging Peter and his shipmates to have faith, is really a copy – or an adaptation – of a vanished original. It was done in mosaic at the turn of the fourteenth century, but was transplanted and restored beyond recognition in the seventeenth. Not a huge amount has been written about the mosaics, though they have been the subject of passing criticism for years (Stendhal, one of the more pungent commentators on the basilica, wrote in *Promenades dans Rome* that 'If ever the idea of finishing off St Peter's arose, all the bad pictures in mosaic would have to be replaced'). Students of the technique will find plenty to engage them, but those of us who like to see a brushstroke here and there will inevitably feel unengaged, if not actually disappointed. Yet even in the absence of copious art-historical debate it seems pretty clear what the Fabbrica was up to. We have seen how full the basilica is of allusions, both filial and antagonistic, to classical antiquity. On a more practical note, we also have seen how its marshy site affected its architectural history. Such a site also meant oil paintings were at risk from the humidity of the air. Reviving and, as far as the aesthetic preferences of the period were concerned, perfecting an ancient Roman (in fact Hellenistic) pictorial technique was very much in keeping with the wider project of rebuilding the basilica. The proverbial longevity of mosaic, a technique in which colours have remained undimmed for many centuries, must also have sat well with the Fabbrica's goals for an undimmed, thousand-year future.

As for the issues of originality and authenticity which weigh so heavily on the post-Romantic visitor, who likes his artists to bridle self-expressively against the bonds of tradition, all that can really be said is that such things carried less weight in the eighteenth century, when most of the mosaics were made. Indeed the artistic culture of that time was all about imitation and tradition, with only certain overwhelmingly gifted individuals given much licence to be individualistic at all. The basilica's claims to greatness certainly partly resided in the idea that it was a model for other religious builders to follow (*matrice* in the words of the Codex Chigi – see Chapter 1). They also resided, paradoxically to us maybe, in the notion that it was itself the result of a process of imitation, a kind of quintessence. It was, in other words, the fruit of a longstanding and cumulative progress towards artistic consensus. The mosaics certainly didn't defer to the paintings on which they were based (the supersizing of the Raphael being a case in point). Still, there is something hygienic and impassive about them. To modern eyes they reinforce the general sense of unrelieved perfection which the Fabbrica and the Sampietrini work so hard to achieve.

All of which is partly a preamble to saying that this chapter will not be listing the works of art dotted around St Peter's in detail. The plan on page xvi–xvii is, I hope, a reasonably comprehensive guide. I have instead singled out a few works which seemed to me to illustrate aspects of the basilica's use, to reinforce some of the broader cultural messages noted elsewhere in the book, or even – in one case – to subvert them. The artistic iconography of St Peter's is anyway not particularly unconventional for a prestigious Catholic church of the sixteenth or seventeenth centuries. There are Early Christian martyrs galore, such as Poussin's St Erasmus having his insides wheeled out of him on a windlass, and the chaste St Petronilla (Peter's daughter according to some sources), whose round shrine once stood alongside the basilica, in a large composition by Guercino. A dome frescoed by Lanfranco shows a crucifix borne aloft in a vertiginous triumph. The chunky mosaics above the four main corner piers depict the four Evangelists, the Gospels being the foundations of the faith just as Matthew, Mark, Luke and John seem now to prop up the abstract, celestial space symbolised by the dome. The gigantic sculpted figures gesticulating from niches in the corner piers advertise the four most prestigious relics housed in the basilica, installed by Bernini in St Veronica's pier. St Peter and St Paul crop up here and there, unsurprisingly, as do several Popes performing miracles or feats of derring-do, like the occasion when Leo IV halted Attila the Hun at the very gates of Rome (here, in a vivid marble relief by Alessandro Algardi, Peter and Paul back the Pope up in person).

The unique thing about St Peter's is the tombs it contains. Unlike other *anciens régimes*, the papacy was not based on the hereditary principle. Popes' paths to the chair of Peter were varied and uncertain – generalship, theological acumen, political ruthlessness, a plausible air of innocence, dead men's shoes. St Peter's has given just a few of the Popes of the last 500 years or so a chance to offer posterity a glimpse of their personalities as they wished them to be seen. What has determined who got the prestigious spaces in the basilica and who was relegated to the Grottoes is not entirely clear. Some

Popes paid for their tombs while they were still alive, though that didn't always guarantee them a prime site – and some Popes managed to wield at least some influence over the choice of their successor, who might then repay the favour posthumously. Certainly it's striking who isn't there. John Paul II currently seems to be about the most famous and popular pontiff since Sylvester I, but languishes modestly in the basement; while Pius IX, who won the principle of papal infallibility at the First Vatican Council in 1870 but lost the Temporal Power to Garibaldi's troops just a few weeks later, was diverted to a simple tomb in San Lorenzo fuori le Mura after nationalists threatened to hijack his funeral procession and toss the corpse into the Tiber.

By their tombs, then, shall we not necessarily know them. In which case some of the grandest tombs nowadays look like something of a hostage to fortune. Canova's elaborate neo-classical memorial to the Venetian Pope Clement XIII shows his gifts off well – intense naturalism in the praying Pope's face, a remarkable ability to suggest different textures in the unforgiving medium of white Carrara marble, a rare talent for lions (there are two: Strength, awake, and Meekness, asleep). But it will have many visitors running to their guide-books to find out who Clement XIII was and what he did. To which the answer is: not a huge amount, though his appoint-ment eased a long disenchantment between the Papal States and the Most Serene Venetian Republic, one reason why his family hired a Venetian sculptor to carve his tomb. He did fight the rulers of Catholic Europe to preserve the increas-ingly controversial Society of Jesus, by a wide margin the most influential organisation in the Catholic world at the time; but his successor, Clement XIV, caved in and suppressed the

Order with a 'breve' headed *Dominus ac Redemptor* in 1773. His tomb is by Canova too: it's in the church of the Most Holy Apostles.

Conversely, one looks around in vain for some of the most celebrated or notorious incumbents such as Sixtus V, who preferred Santa Maria Maggiore for his final repose; and Julius II, of course, has his tomb in another St Peter's, San Pietro in Vincoli, though his remains are in the Vatican basilica alongside those of his uncle, Sixtus IV. No trace whatever seems to remain of the epically villanous Borgia Pope Alexander VI, who was subjected to a *damnatio memoriae* or a posthumous sending-to-Coventry by his successors, though he was ultimately responsible for Michelangelo's *Pietà*, and more directly for some charming and historically informative frescoes by Pinturicchio in the Vatican Palace. In fact Alexander's most appropriate epitaph might be this, one of the first pasquinades (the statue where these were mainly posted was only dug up a year before his death):

> Tortures, intrigues, violence, frenzy, anger, lust;
> Rome was a sponge for my cruelty and blood!
> Here lies Alexander the Sixth: Rome, breathe free;
> My death means life for you.

– which might not look well incised into the glassy surface of a grand marble sarcophagus in the Apostle's basilica. Meanwhile a favourite Pope of mine, Prospero Lambertini, enthroned in 1740 as Benedict XIV, is remembered in an unoriginal and unremarkable effort by Pietro Bracci. Benedict wasn't a hugely industrious patron at St Peter's, though he commissioned the silver casket where the palliums spend the night of 28 June.

But he was the nearest thing to an Enlightenment figure to sit in Peter's chair. He allowed the Habsburg empress Maria Theresa to extend religious freedom to Protestants – though not to Jews – living under her rule, and Voltaire dedicated *Mohammed* to him. His mirthful nature is best illustrated by his wish that anybody who said 'Cazzo!' ('Cock!') ten times in one day ought to be rewarded with a plenary indulgence. But you wouldn't know any of that from Bracci's tomb.

Inevitably, though, many of the most important Popes in the history of St Peter's have managed to secure themselves the most conspicuous tombs in the building. One dramatic pairing is Paul III and Urban VIII. Paul, the Farnese Pope, was the man who brought Michelangelo to work on the basilica in 1546. His tomb was done in a fair stab at Michelangelo's style by Guglielmo della Porta. A bronze seated figure of the Pope sits on a high platform, framed by two allegorical female figures lounging on marble scrolls in a clear reference to Michelangelo's Medici tombs in Florence, begun a few years before (and assembled by students after Michelangelo's return to Rome) but never finished. There were originally four figures, when the tomb stood more freely out from the wall in its original location; Bernini moved it to where it is now, just to the left of the tribune, and used it as a jumping-off point for his own monument to Urban VIII, his first employer at St Peter's, which inhabits the niche to the right of the Cathedra. Bernini's respect for della Porta's Michelangelesque prototype is as immediately apparent as his rivalry with it. His tomb has the same seated Pope, same high base, same pair of allegorical figures, same Medici Chapel scrolls, but everything is subtly inflated and enhanced. Urban still has his tiara on, giving him something of a height advantage over his predecessor. He is also caught in the expansive act of benediction rather than sitting pensively as does Paul. The two female figures in Bernini's tomb, representing Charity and Justice, stand, or rather lean, against the outer edges of a black marble sarcophagus instead of reclining along its sloping sides. Charity is attended by a wriggling cohort of babies. They frame a shrouded skeleton who is depicted in the act of inscribing Urban's name on a gilt-bronze tablet, still only partly attached to the tomb's base. Most striking of all is Bernini's use of coloured marble to differentiate the elements of the tomb and animate the whole.

Even more elaborate is the tomb Bernini later designed – one might almost say 'choreographed' – for Alexander VII, awkwardly situated on the south side of the basilica in a niche pierced by a doorway (Fig. 13). Bernini took the composition of his earlier tomb and gave it still more movement and variety. Four figures now crowd round the elevated figure of the Pope, in postures of lamentation. He kneels above them in pious prayer. The two foreground figures are Charity (again, though this time with just the one baby) and Truth, trampling on Heresy as symbolised by the British Isles (that snakepit of Protestants and regicides) on a small globe underfoot. Across the top of the doorway they brandish the tomb's great *coup de théâtre*, a billowing drapery, made by cementing a veneer of red jasper over a carved lump of travertine (an assistant carted a life-size clay model all the way to the quarries in Tivoli to find the right piece of stone). The skeleton from Urban's tomb is back, this time clutching an hourglass and struggling to shimmy itself free from the enveloping drapery. The overall message (the word often used of Bernini's allegories is *concetto*, concept or conceit)

13. The tomb of Alexander VII by Bernini. The heavy, jasper-faced curtain
billowing underneath the seated pontiff is said to represent the Flesh, one of
the things over which Alexander's virtuous deeds will enable him to triumph.
The sensuality of marbles and other coloured stones makes them highly
adaptable to symbolic purposes (see Chapter 4).

is that the good deeds of the Pope will guarantee his fame, ensure his salvation and thereby vanquish the Grim Reaper. In this there seems something felicitous or even opportunistic about the placement of the door, which comes to stand for the very threshold of Death (rather than the doorway to an ante-room leading to a spiral staircase in the thickness of the walls, which is what it actually is).

The unembarrassed emotionalism and busy forms of Bernini's two tombs were strongly influential on only a few of his successors, though they harmonise as well as you'd expect with other aspects of his work at St Peter's: the polychromy, the gesticulating figures, the large scale. Later critics would see them as ridiculously affected. J. J. Winckelmann, one of the first and most influential advocates of neoclassicism, wrote that Bernini had 'singlehandedly ... introduced corruption into art'. Sir Joshua Reynolds inveighed against Bernini's sculpture, warning students at the Royal Academy that he had 'strayed from the right path', and complaining that the drapery clothing his figures never had anything to do with the body beneath. A sweetness of effect noted by Bernini's contemporaries – the Italian word used is *morbidezza*, softness or tenderness – was too much for the ascetic palettes of the nineteenth century. Stendhal found Bernini's work at St Peter's '*pretty*, and thus little worthy of this temple which is *beautiful*'. He also felt that the four colossal statues at the crossing (only one of which is by Bernini) ought to be shipped off to America, where the uneducated middle classes could enjoy their sentimentality. Meanwhile for John Ruskin, as we've seen, Bernini represented the nadir of post-Raphaelite schmaltz. But nowadays Bernini is back in vogue. Scholars of the mid-twentieth century found in the

Italian Baroque a long-untapped seam of art-historical ore. There was a new curiosity about the elaborate allegories used by artists of the seventeenth century. Taste followed a few steps behind academic interest. Bernini, unlike Caravaggio, say, was never going to appeal to admirers of realism: nor to those high modernists who identified in Poussin a kind of encrypted abstraction. But *morbidezza* has become admissible again lately. Bernini looks from here like an artist of empathy and sensibility, a Baroque rose between the rationalist thorns of the Renaissance and neoclassicism. Postmodernists in the late twentieth century loved his gusto and complexity. He could be appreciated as a master technician, producing works which seem to hover or to fly, which defy the limitations of material and structure; or as a prototypical magic-realist, a fabulist, a relayer of marvels. It is easy to overlook how miraculous some of Bernini's arrangements must once have seemed, even if such concrete expressions of religious mysteries have become less and less central to modern believers. Theatrical metaphors are widely and somewhat lazily applied to his work (though he did write and put on plays at the Vatican court, despite there being nothing so ungodly as a purpose-built theatre there). The sense one sometimes gets from his sculpture of implausible things being made to happen in unlikely places must have spoken to an appetite for wonder, novelty and caprice, grounded always in an emphatic emotional realism, which was forged by his contemporaries' experience of drama, religious or allegorical, as much as any expectations they may have had of 'pure' visual art. We have seen in Chapter 4 how certain degrees of religious belief might inflect on the concept of allegory or even the very convention of artistic representation: that faith might make a work of art really become that which it symbolised, just as the Host really becomes the body of Christ.

Other papal tombs are less arresting, though Pollaiuolo's bronze tomb of Innocent VIII in the left-hand aisle, transplanted from Old St Peter's, is worth seeking out if you want a glimpse of the explicitly classicising imagery of the late fifteenth century, not to mention the virtuosity of fifteenth-century Florentine casting and chasing techniques (another Pollaiuolo tomb, that of Innocent's predecessor Sixtus IV, is in the Treasury, an ad hoc museum of various supernumerary items from St Peter's, reached by a passage near the Innocent tomb – see the plan on pages xvi–xvii).

The proposition that the past century or so has seen the tide of papal artistic patronage growing somewhat becalmed is only feebly challenged by the most recent papal memorial to find space in the basilica itself, that of Pius XII, Pope during the troubled and compromised war years and the presiding force behind the excavations of the necropolis, whose body lies below in the Grottoes, but who is commemorated in a bronze statue by Francesco Messina, unveiled in 1964. This looms alarmingly out at the passers-by in exaggerated imitation of Alexander VII further along. It echoes the sprinkling of monuments erected to twentieth-century Popes on the opposite side of the basilica, including Benedict XV, who opposed the First World War rather more forcefully than Pius XII did the Second World War, and John XXIII, who convened the Second Vatican Council. All these representations are in the pockmarked, mildly expressionistic style of much modern bronze sculpture. A couple of them wrestle gamely with one of the most urgent representational problems confronting sculptors of the last couple of centuries, namely spectacles.

The difficulty of representing these in marble, as opposed to bronze, is evident in a statue erected recently in a niche outside the church. It commemorates the controversial saint Jose Maria d'Escriva, founder in 1928 of Opus Dei, 'God's Work'. You can see it on your right as you go through the corridor leading to the Treasury. D'Escriva was fast-tracked to sainthood by Pope John Paul II. He was canonised in 2002, despite scant evidence of the requisite miracle-working skills. But Opus Dei, ostensibly a lay organisation dedicated to the 'sanctification' of work and family, and boasting several wealthy and influential members, has also become a powerful stratum in the Catholic hierarchy. Several members or fellow-travellers were given important posts in the Church during John Paul II's papacy. In South America their conservatism helped to contain the liberation-theology movement, whose members had been exhibiting an elastic approach to dogma reminiscent of the Jesuits in their prime, expressing left-wing views and even sometimes turning a blind eye to official Catholic policy on contraception and other 'social' – that is to say sexual – issues. John Paul II, who had battled against secular Communism in Eastern Europe throughout his earlier career, was doubtless impressed by d'Escriva's similarly hardline stance. But d'Escriva had supported Franco, and has been quoted as saying, 'The Hitler who was against the Jews and the Slavs was the same Hitler who was against the communists,' which is stretching most accepted definitions of a conservative. But it is not so much the political alignment of Opus Dei as its secretive nature, not to mention its members' mild flagellant tendencies, which have made the organisation so notorious, most recently in Dan Brown's gigaton-selling potboiler *The Da Vinci Code*.

Several new statues have started to sprout in these external niches, though they're not always accessible to the public. They speak of the revived fortunes of the Church in Eastern Europe after the collapse of the Soviet system, and in the developing world. Most of them are pretty grim from an artistic standpoint, but they do emphatically demonstrate the last Pope's policy of supporting and recognising the growth of the Church in the territories where it was growing fastest, and letting Western Europe and the United States take care of themselves for a while. In fact, most of his architectural patronage, apart from the cleaning and restoration work undertaken for the 2000 Jubilee, was far away from the Vatican, in the poor and multi-ethnic outskirts of Rome and in churches with a particular affiliation to this or that country.

A few of the tombs inside St Peter's are not dedicated to Popes. We have seen how the mortal remains of Matilda of Canossa were brought by Urban VIII to Rome as righteous plunder from his campaign against the duchy of Mantua. More intriguing is a pair of tombs placed near the entrance to the basilica, set in corresponding positions on the right and left aisle. These commemorate two small victories won by the Catholic Church against heresy in two of its most forceful strongholds, Sweden and England. Queen Christina of Sweden ('That Dreadful Woman', as A.J.P. Taylor called her) was a child of six in 1632 when her father Gustavus II Adolphus died on the battlefield, almost halfway through the Thirty Years' War. Nobody's Protestantism had raged more furiously than his, so Christina's later abdication, conversion to Catholicism and relocation to Rome was quite a scalp for the True Church. Leaving aside the fact that Christina was explicitly spared any of the tedious acts of worship normally expected of a practising Catholic, and the suspicion that the whole thing was a diplomatic wheeze cooked up by Axel Oxenstierna, Sweden's canny Regent and Chancellor, it is unsurprising that the 'Queen of the Swedes, the Goths and the Vandals', as she is called on her tomb, has been so celebrated. The tomb, by Jean-Baptiste Théodon, is not wildly exciting from an aesthetic point of view. But if you want to see the remains of the woman who supposedly precipitated the death of René Descartes by making him wait in draughty Scandinavian passages before teaching her – here they are (or rather, beneath here in the Grottoes is where the actual remains are).

Symmetry is a pervasive organising principle in St Peter's – and another thing which the basilica's huge scale tends to disguise. One's progress round the building entails changes of scope and focus, sudden shifts from the general to the particular and back again. It also takes a while to do the full circuit, so dialogues between pairs of monuments can easily be overlooked. But Christina's tomb is clearly meant to rhyme with another memorial on the south aisle, politically if not aesthetically. This is by Canova, almost as well represented in St Peter's as Bernini, and commemorates James, Charles and Henry Stuart, all buried in the Grottoes beneath (James's estranged wife Maria Clementina Sobieska is represented by a mosaic portrait nearby). Of these, the least prominent in Rome was the best-known in Britain: Charles, the Young Pretender or Bonnie Prince Charlie. Ever since James

VI of Scotland became James I of England in 1603 after the death of his cousin Elizabeth I, the Stuarts had struck British Protestants as having what later generations would call a whiff of incense about them. When Charles I built a Catholic chapel for his wife Henrietta Maria, it looked very much to some English Protestants like treason; when his son Charles II accepted money from Louis XIV of France to defray the expenses of his proverbially saucy court (which pretty much was treason), religious paranoia was inflamed along with political indignation. The Stuarts would impose Catholicism and despotism – the two terms being seen as all but interchangeable – on us all.

By the middle of the eighteenth century, the Stuarts had been ousted, the Scottish and English crowns united and the German – and impeccably Protestant – house of Hanover was settled securely on the throne. Charles Stuart was heavily defeated by a Hanoverian army at the Battle of Culloden in 1745, an event which has since enjoyed surprising resonance among nationalist Scots given that more of their forefathers took the Hanoverian than the Stuart side. Charles's brother Henry became a cardinal two years later, an event which probably did the family's chances of restoration more harm than the 'Forty-Five' itself. Their father James passed a long and melancholy old age in Rome, sipping broth before Mass by a papal dispensation last granted to the Habsburg emperor Charles V.

After the death of the Old Pretender in 1766, the papal authorities voted not to recognise Charles as the rightful ruler of Britain. This was Realpolitik rather than a personal judgement on Charles. Britain had been allies of the victorious Prussian side in the Seven Years' War, concluded in 1763.

In 1764, several high-ranking papal officials had received Edward Augustus, the Hanoverian Duke of York, travelling incognito in Rome on a Grand Tour, and the Pope himself had made him a gift of Piranesi etchings. During Edward's visit Henry, the Stuart Duke of York, had been encouraged to make himself scarce. Nevertheless, Rome remained for many British visitors not only the toxic fountainhead of Papism but the bolt-hole of the Jacobites, supporters of a Catholic (and therefore despotic) Stuart succession. There was no regular British diplomatic presence there. Horace Mann, the ambassador to the Grand Duchy of Tuscany just to the north, wrote regular dispatches back to the Secretary of State, reporting on the Stuarts, where they went and whom they met. In 1770 we catch a glimpse of the embittered and alcoholic Young Pretender, not so young any more, asserting one last inalienable monarchical franchise, the legendary ability to cure skin diseases by the laying on of hands: 'two or three very low people have applied to him to be touched for scrofulous disorders, which service he performed'.

By the time Henry died in 1807 feelings about Jacobitism back in Britain had waned somewhat. A forceful anti-Catholicism is still evidenced by the Gordon riots of 1780, but the colossal impact of the French Revolution and its Napoleonic aftershock made old anxieties about the doctrine of *cuius regio, eius religio* seem a little old-fashioned. *The Times* even gave Henry a kindly obituary: 'The Cardinal of York … early dedicated himself to a life congenial with the habits of his mind.' Certainly relations with the Hanoverians had thawed. Henry left the Stuart regalia to the Prince Regent. George III had paid Henry a pension from 1800, and on his death chipped in 50,000 francs to a subscription raised for the St Peter's monument by his executors (though Canova noted that more was promised but never appeared). Canova's tomb became something of a diplomatic triumph. The Hanoverians could appear magnanimous in victory; the papal authorities steadfast in their – increasingly nostalgic – adherence to a very different model of kingship.

It helped that the tomb was judged such an artistic success (Fig. 14). It is a compact marble trapezium inspired by Roman altars and the tombs modelled on them. The three Stuarts are portrayed in profile on the upper part of the structure, while the Royal Standard occupies the stubby pediment above. The lower part consists of a barely open door framed by two ephebic youths, who were partly draped following an early complaint from the Pope's major-domo, one Monsignor Frosini, but whose heavy, epicene bottoms still seem to carry a slightly heavier patina than the rest of the monument, as if many classically inclined visitors had drawn a dreamy finger across them in some private ritual down the years.

The hard-to-please Stendhal said that Michelangelo himself had done only one thing as good as the Stuart memorial: his figure of Moses on the Julius tomb in San Pietro in Vincoli. That opinion relegates the most popular single work of art at St Peter's, the *Pietà*, to a secondary status which would strike most modern visitors as wrongheaded to say the least (Fig. 12). Commissioned in 1499 by Cardinal Bilhères de Lagraulas, the French ambassador to the court of Alexander VI, Michelangelo's early masterpiece takes the placid idealism of the Italian High Renaissance – no livid scars or howls of grief here – as its point of departure. The improbable youth of the Virgin Mary, and the considerable heft of the dead Christ sprawled across her lap – though Smollett said

IACOBO·III
IACOBI·II·MAGNAE·BRIT·REGIS·FILIO
KAROLO·EDVARDO
ET·HENRICO·DECANO·PATRVM·CARDINALIVM
IACOBI·III·FILIIS
REGIAE·STIRPIS·STVARDIAE·POSTREMIS
ANNO·M·DCCC·XIX

14. The Stuart monument by Canova, 1819. Canova's classicising aesthetic makes this an odd intruder in the largely baroque interior of the church. The tomb seems to concede a simple solemnity to death, in contrast to Bernini's colourful allegories in which death is gloriously trampled underfoot.

he looked 'as if he had died of a consumption' – do nothing to undermine the sculpture. Rather a clever conical composition makes Christ's body seem balanced and stable, and the angelic features of Mary universalise the work's powerful emotional message. Something of its tenderness and grace is even preserved in the miniature resin copies knocked out by Rome's industrious souvenir-makers, which is quite an achievement.

The *Pietà* has been shifted round a few times since its creation, from the chapel of St Petronilla beside the old basilica, to a spot on the left of the nave, to the choir chapel (it sat at a neck-craning height on top of an altar, and could not be seen when the chapel was in use). Its present location dates back to the eighteenth century, and its elegant oval base to Francesco Borromini in the seventeenth. The stark marble cross on the wall behind follows the template of an old Carolingian crucifix, and Giovanni Lanfranco's fresco of the Triumph of the Cross (now almost the only painting to be seen in St Peter's) decorates the vault above. Religious visitors are therefore asked to see Michelangelo's sculpture in the context of some fairly abstract imagery about the incarnation and Passion of Christ – yet its status as a work of art can make it seem above and beyond all questions of 'context' at all.

In fact, it is an interesting thought-experiment to ask oneself whether something which seems by fairly broad acclamation to represent one of Western civilisation's more impressive achievements is better or worse at concentrating the minds of the faithful than something less artistically successful. Anybody beginning to study art history is quickly taught that works of art change their meaning over time, and that recovering the 'period eye' can be more problematic than it sometimes seems (more problematic than a recent slew of novels about famous artists of the past would suggest, at any rate). We can usually tell what religious art was originally for – a Bible for the illiterate, a trigger for prayer, a lesson in the physical reality of martyrdom. A late medieval bronze statue of St Peter, cautiously attributed to Arnolfo di Cambio, sits in a *sedia gestatoria* at the foot of the pier of St Longinus at St Peter's. It is hard to work up too much of a sweat about as a work of art, but has attracted rather more devoted tactile attention from visitors than even the winged young men on the Stuart monument. The acidic sweat of millions of hands grasping the foot in the hope of a blessing has blurred the apostle's foot away into a dully reflective tongue of metal. Similar things may well have happened to the Michelangelo in its time (though it's securely glassed in now after it was vandalised in 1972). But high artistic regard does seem to muffle a work of religious art's religiosity, not least because any genuine pilgrim would have to fight his way past a ruck of tourists to get close to such an object. It may be that the inverse also applies, and an intense aura of religious potency, like that surrounding the relic of the blood of St Januarius in Naples, say, makes would-be connoisseurs bashful about seeing the reliquary chapel from a purely aesthetic point of view, though some have tried to say that the aesthetic and the religious are really just different aspects of the same thing. The question is acutely relevant to St Peter's because the church is forever crowded with visitors pursuing very different agendas. The tourists inconvenience the faithful, while the faithful baffle the tourists. Of course, many in the church at a given moment will be both tourist and pilgrim. But that doesn't make it any easier to pray to the *Pietà*, or to cast a coolly cultured eye over Bernini and Borromini's exquisite work – a ciborium, modelled on Bramante's Tempietto, by the former, a wrought-iron gate by the latter – in the Chapel of the Holy Sacrament, which is reserved for prayer by Sampietrini who guard the entrance with the zeal of nightclub bouncers.

Certainly, the works of art at St Peter's are intended to do many different things; and some of them may have ended up doing both more and less than intended. Tombs are, I should have thought, difficult to see metaphysically for most people these days, but serve as informative historical documents and essays in this or that artistic style. Saints depicted on altar-pieces or in statues preserve their original, devotional function, but may be judged by more worldly criteria too. Giant arm-waving statues do what ordinary mortals cannot do, and throw some kind of enlivening human presence out into the immensity of the basilica. Mosaics make painting somehow a little more like architecture, and strike the sort of ambitious ecumenical note often sought by papal patrons, looking simultaneously a little bit classical and a little bit Byzantine.

We could do worse than to finish our promenade around the inside of the basilica where we began it, by the doors. Here architecture and sculpture, ritual and temporal power all collide. The loggia or vestibule which runs across the façade of St Peter's is a useful functional space in that it allows those entering and exiting the basilica to be segregated. The window from which the Pope gives his blessing to the city and the world is above. The vault of the loggia was decorated with stucco reliefs in the time of Maderno, though Bernini also inserted a marble relief of Christ asking Peter to feed his sheep – that's us, of course. At each end is an arch opening on to a dramatic equestrian statue: Cornacchini's Charlemagne from 1724–5 to the south, Bernini's Constantine, unveiled in 1670, to the north (Fig. 15). The significance of the two emperors is clear; the two commissions were among the last attempts the Popes would make to associate themselves with imperial power. Bernini's figure in particular shows all his characteristic dynamism of form and ingenuity with light, with the force of Constantine's conversion cleverly expressed by the natural light drawn down to strike the figure from above.

Because the site slopes down from north to south, the two statues fit rather differently into the framing architecture. Charlemagne sits in a little niche on one end of the façade, while Constantine is actually just beyond the end of the loggia, from which he is visible through a glass door. The north wing of Bernini's colonnade terminates in a grand staircase, the Scala Regia, along which princely guests to the Vatican used to climb. Putting Constantine in their path was an unmistakable reminder of the Popes' claim to be kingmakers, and the imperial sanction from which papal power had drawn its often all too shaky legitimacy. The two emperors are possibly also a ghostly reminder of the two towers which stood over the narthex of Old St Peter's between which, in a chapel called Santa Maria inter Turres, the Emperor used to swear an oath of loyalty to the Pope. Bernini's attempts to build two towers on the façade of New St Peter's failed in the 1640s when the soft site got the better of him and his south tower started to pull the façade itself out of true; but memories of the old basilica remained intense and urgent in the new one, and the choice to locate two imperial statues at the foot of where the new towers ought to have stood must have been a knowing one. It seems that no plans were ever

15. Constantine the Great, by Bernini, 1654–70, seen from the portico. The position of the statue makes the morning light strike it in a clever echo of Constantine's Christian revelation in 312. The sculpture stands at a point of intersection between the basilica and the Scala Regia, the main processional entrance into the Vatican palace, and so has something to say about the *temporale*, the Popes' princely power, though this was definitively on the wane when the statue was made.

mooted to cannibalise the benediction loggia and fashion a new Santa Maria inter Turres; though the pastoral function exercised by the giving of blessings to large groups of the faithful might be said to have grown in importance as the Pope's temporal power waned – look at John Paul II, who made his name speaking up against political power and for the People.

The five rectangular openings into the loggia from the piazza are aligned with five doors which lead into the basilica itself. These all have special names and ritual functions. The Holy Door near the Michelangelo has the most peculiar ritual function of all, which is not to be a door most of the time. Ordinarily it is walled up, but every Jubilee year it is ritually demolished by the Sampietrini, after the Pope has given it a ceremonial tap with a hammer. The message is that in these special years more pilgrims will visit, and freer access to the church will be extended to them (until the mid-twentieth century there was no door there at all, just a space during the Jubilee, and a wall the rest of the time). The first Jubilee was in 1300, called by Pope Boniface VIII, one of the great innovators in the field of papal ritual. Its probable purpose was to capitalise on the inaccessibility of the Holy Land and lure a bumper crop of pilgrims to Rome. Unfortunately, the papal court moved to Avignon just five years later, but Jubilees have been called on the century, or the half- or quarter-century, ever since. Pilgrims who attend Mass in any of the seven ancient churches get a full remission of all sins committed to date – not a bad deal.

Five doors makes more sense in the context of the old building, with its double aisles and central nave – and the oldest of the working doors, the central one, is a relic from the previous basilica. It is decorated with delicate Early Renaissance reliefs by Antonio Averlino, who called himself Filarete, the lover of wisdom. These set Christian narratives, most conspicuously the crucifixion of Peter between two *metae*, side-by-side with modern scenes of papal statecraft such as the crowning of Sigismund II by Eugenius IV in 1433, and the ecumenical council called by the same Pope in Florence eight years later. Surrounding the panels are twirling passages of vegetable and classical ornament, though some were put on afterwards when the door was enlarged to fit the new church. Filarete's doors make a strong contrast with the so-called Door of Death, the southernmost entrance to the basilica, carried out by Giacomo Manzù in an expressionistic style not a million miles away from that of Francis Bacon or Alberto Giacometti. The reliefs are very much informed by the recent raw experiences of the Second World War. Not much compositional or stylistic distinction is drawn between pacific and even celebratory death scenes such as the Assumption of the Virgin and more violent martyrdoms like the stoning of St Stephen or the murder of Abel by Cain. Isolated, stylised figures gesticulate and howl on stark, slightly roughened bronze squares. It's powerful stuff, perhaps the most successful modern art to be seen in the Vatican (though the Vatican museums have a collection of modern religious art, including one of Bacon's famous variations on Velasquez's portrait of Innocent X).

The doors either side of the centre are called the Door of Good and Evil and the Door of the Sacraments. Both date from the mid-twentieth century. The former has a representation of the Second Vatican Council (also depicted on the back of Manzù's door), held in 1962–5 on the orders of John

XXIII. This was an event of crucial importance in post-war Catholicism, leading among other things to the adoption of different vernacular languages in place of the Latin Mass composed at the Council of Trent some four centuries before (though the Tridentine Mass, as it's called, is still often used at St Peter's and elsewhere). It is tempting to see Manzù, and the other twentieth-century sculptors who worked on the doors, as expressing some clerical Zeitgeist, just as artists like Caravaggio and Bernini are said to have given visual expression to post-Tridentine Catholicism in its austere earlier and triumphant later stage. If so then these must have been dour and uncertain times. After the war the loyalty of Catholics, and especially Italian Catholics, to the Church and its leadership was still steadfast. Plenty of good deeds on the part of Pius XII during the war could be cited, though it has since been claimed that he could or should have done – and certainly said – more (unlike Benedict XV, who had spoken out tirelessly against the First World War, perhaps one reason why Joseph Ratzinger chose to call himself Benedict XVI). But Italy was exhausted, depopulated and impoverished – and the legacy of Mussolini, who had said early on in his regime that he hated both the Christianity of Christ and that of Marx, before making an opportunistic conversion to the delight of the Pope, would continue to be divisive. In 1949 Pius excommunicated all Communists – a slap in the face for the leftist partisans who had fought Hitler and Mussolini so tirelessly just a few years before. Borrowing a well-known bon mot about the French Revolution, it's perhaps too early to say what the Second Vatican Council was all about. It coincided with the social changes of the sixties, and provided the Church with a soapbox from which to proclaim its social conservatism, a stance it has maintained ever since (though the liberation-theology movement in Latin America and elsewhere has sometimes had other ideas). But many of the changes wrought by the Council were essentially administrative. Even allowing priests to say Mass in the vernacular has its administrative aspect; and the question of whether cardinals need to be bishops, for example, may not set pulses racing any more. But the fact that the Council is commemorated in such a prominent place in St Peter's – next to the Council of Florence, indeed – implies that in the early sixties the Church felt a strong urge at least to appear modern. And the cast of that modernity was distressed, weary and tragic. Of course, the interior of the basilica stayed the same: a metaphor for the long entirety of Christian history, and a glimpse of Paradise on earth. And most visitors, sadly, don't even stop to look at the doors on the way in or out.

7

··

PERSPECTIVES

I asked the brick what it wanted and it said, I want to be an arch.

Louis Kahn

Buildings like St Peter's ingest, process and excrete us as though we were plankton. Our illusion of choices exercised and curiosities pursued seems vain and trivial compared to our speck-like size, or to an organisation of space and spectacle which demands little of us beyond awe and obedience. This is a well-worn path in the history of architecture, and the terms applied to it are nowadays often critical: imperialist, megalomaniac, fascist. But as Fontana and many other 'official' chroniclers of St Peter's make clear, it is a central part of the visitor's intended experience of the church. Through its doors you are not so much induced as inhaled, over the *rota* towards the baldacchino: from there, to gasp at the magnitude of the crossing and the pier statues; you perceive (a little dimly) that this sudden immersion in the vertical involves an opening downwards as well as upwards, that the building is chthonic as well as celestial. Then and only then do you start to look around you: at the tombs, the marble, the inscriptions running round the frieze. You pace from chapel to chapel. You mark out the space, both physically and perceptually, see how it looks from different angles. You begin to feel like a more active participant in your visit.

After such an experience, in which unconscious submission gives way to a more conscious and even critical engagement, there is a primitive delight in climbing up on to the roof of St Peter's. Having been inside, you are striving again to be outside. The building which has enfolded and sought to overwhelm you is just a stepping-stone to enjoy some stunning views of Rome and Lazio. Some of its secrets are disclosed to you on the way. There is even a bar on the roof.

The best things in life aren't always free, though, and there is currently a small charge to climb the stairs, and a slightly less small one to use the lift. The lift you go up in was installed by John Paul II, one of his few works at St Peter's. The project is commemorated in Latin at the top. *Ascensum in templi fastigium expediendum curavit* – he saw to making the climb to the summit of the temple easier. The stairs are buried in the thick outer walls of the basilica (in fact there are several spiral flights dotted around the church, pleasingly called *lumache* – snails – in Italian).

The aisles of St Peter's are roofed by a series of gently-sloping brick pavements. The higher domes capping the westernmost pair of chapels, the choir and the Chapel of the Most Holy Sacrament, as well as Michelangelo's main dome itself – protrude above the terracotta like a pair of sea anemones at low tide, while the others lie several metres below in rectangular light-wells. A higher, pitched ridge along the central spine of the building signals the tunnel-vaulted nave within. It is nestling in the eaves of this that the visitor can slake his or her thirst with a small but welcome range of non-alcoholic drinks and ice-creams. Next to the bar there is even a little shop, staffed by nuns in livery of intense blue, selling souvenirs and religious paraphernalia.

Already at this level the views are impressive. There is also a sense of being able for the first time to appreciate the sheer bulk of the building, the thickness of the walls, the vast blocks of travertine used to face the outside and the unimaginable tonnage of rubble, concrete and brick within. The statues of Christ and the Apostles which crown the façade are visible from behind, crudely carved as if from some kind of cheese, as are the nippled tiaras crowning the two elaborate clocks designed by Giuseppe Valadier in the early eighteenth century. But only the fainthearted stop at the roof, though this is where the backpackers pause to sunbathe on hot days. The principal summit is still overhead: Michelangelo's dome (Fig. 16).

Given that most of Michelangelo's work inside St Peter's has been more or less obliterated, and what one can see of his walls is best seen from the hard-to-access Vatican gardens behind, the dome is by far his most conspicuous surviving achievement at the basilica. Even so, there has been extensive academic speculation over how far the built dome diverges from Michelangelo's designs. As we saw in Chapter 3, Bramante's proposal for rebuilding the church probably involved a hemispherical dome on the model of the Pantheon. Antonio da Sangallo opted for a parabolic dome – probably for structural reasons – though by wrapping two arcades round the outside of his design he disguised its tallness. Michelangelo left relatively few drawings of his proposals for St Peter's behind. A pair of engravings of 1569 by Etienne Dupérac shows a dome not hugely dissimilar to the one built: two hemispheres sitting snugly together like upside-down tumblers on a shelf. This doubled-up arrangement is derived from Brunelleschi's

16. View of the dome and south-west corner of the church. Whether or not every detail here is really by him, this gives a pretty good sense of Michelangelo's architectural style. The tall pilasters overlap, giving a sense of the outside of the church being folded or pleated. The snarling windows in the attic create a dramatic play of mass and space, light and shadow – and they suggest a blurring of sculpture and architecture (though Michelangelo maybe mooted something simpler). The ribbed dome extends a strong vertical emphasis upwards from the side walls.

treatment of Florence Cathedral, always an influential model on St Peter's. It means a dome can reach the required height outside, but you don't have to stand right underneath it to see its full concavity inside. It also means you can put stairs into the space between the inner and the outer domes. As built, the inner dome is hemispherical while the outer is slightly elliptical. Scholarly argument about the dome, as with other unresolved questions to do with the outside of the church, like whether Michelangelo actually wanted the heavy, pedimented attic windows which now form such a conspicuous element of the exterior of the church, or his assistants made the church look more Michelangelesque than Michelangelo himself would have done, has been intense (see Chapter 4). The starting point is always to ask oneself what works. The general consensus is that the hemispherical inner dome looks better from the inside, while the ovoid outer dome looks better, in the sense of being a shade more prominent, a shade less prone to distortion when seen from far below, and, indeed, a shade more hemispherical, from the outside. Because things have worked out so well, admirers of Michelangelo tend to want to believe he sanctioned it rather than one of his successors, mostly men who didn't completely cover themselves in glory in their own independent careers. But whether we should speak of Michelangelo's dome or Giacomo della Porta and Domenico Fontana's dome, or just see the whole project as so steeped in collaboration and historical dialogue as to be beyond any petty issues of individual authorship at all, must remain a difficult question. Interestingly, it has just come to light that Della Porta's workshop for the dome at St Peter's was the crossing of San Paolo fuori le Mura, at that time the only indoor space big enough to accommodate the full circumference of the job in hand, on the other side of the city. Archaeologists burrowing through the floor of the church in an attempt to verify the identity of the remains buried there, as their predecessors claimed to do for St Peter half a century ago, have found a life-sized template of the St Peter's dome incised on the floor of San Paolo, obscured at least since the fire of 1823. This doesn't tell us much about the intended shape of the dome – it was always going to be round in plan – but it does remind us, among other things, of the powerful symmetries and fraternities which bind together the great churches of Rome.

From the nave and aisle roof, steps take the climber up to the base of the drum, a heavy cylinder girt round with sixteen pairs of Corinthian columns. These make little protruding bunches of masonry which stop the dome above them from spreading outwards under its own weight. They also give a vertical accent to the appearance of the drum, making it seem more stout and sculptural than would the simple row of evenly spaced columns used by Bramante in the Tempietto, and projected by him for St Peter's. From this point the dome is more or less invisible, curving away out of sight overhead. What can be seen are several repaired cracks, each one inscribed with the date of repair. These imply a kind of pride – in the know-how of the Sampietrini, at least – but also constitute a rare confession that St Peter's is not immune to the depredations of time or gravity. We have already seen how difficulties with the site, and inadequacies in the early provision of structural support for the central area of the church, led to rethinks and crises during the sixteenth century. The most spectacular architectural failure in the rebuilt basilica's history was the subsidence of Bernini's bell-tower in 1641.

The cracks this caused in the façade and the benediction loggia within it are inaccessible to the public, but those on the drum are commemorated in the same bashful way. The damage to the dome was also attributed to Bernini, who had excavated niches and stairwells into the corner piers directly below the dome in the late 1620s and 1630s. A book of 1684 on the architecture of St Peter's quotes an exchange between Bernini and Francesco Mochi, who carved the figure of St Veronica in the crossing below. Bernini asked where the wind came from which was causing the *sudarium* or veil of St Veronica, miraculously imprinted with the face of Christ, to billow out so energetically. Mochi answered: 'From the crack you made in the cupola!'

From the drum one is led back inside the church, to a gallery at the base of the dome. Here it is possible to see a vertiginous view down into the basilica, where the baldacchino and the pier statues seem themselves reduced to model-village size – another atavistic pleasure, if primarily one for the strong of stomach. It is also clear from close by how large the tesserae of the dome mosaics are, and how oddly – and not unpleasingly – stylised the four Evangelists above the crossing piers, and the twelve Apostles in the dome itself, appear. The inversion of perspectives creates a dramatic shift in scale, a common enough experience at St Peter's.

Having been a morsel in the belly of the beast, the climber now becomes a parasite, burrowing within its skin, or, more properly, between its skins. The ascent into the dome itself is cramped and disorientating, but it does show a few glimpses of the way the thing is put together. The inner dome is stepped, like the lower part of the Pantheon's. The outer is built around sixteen stone ribs, a trick used by Brunelleschi at Florence Cathedral (which has twenty-four ribs). Most of the material in between is brick. Flights of stairs coil round the dome, converging at the lantern on top. Here one is again ejected, breathlessly, from the building.

The climb up to the dome of St Peter's features in one of the defining documents of post-war Rome, Fellini's *La Dolce Vita*. The actress Sylvia (Anita Ekberg) has donned close-fitting clerical garb for a photo opportunity. The press pack hurl themselves after her up the stairs, gasping inanities. One by one they fall by the wayside until only Marcello (Marcello Mastroianni) is left, bloody but unbowed. The prodigious Sylvia barely breaks sweat before they arrive at the little circular gallery which perches on top of the dome, letting light in and securing the vaulting in place. Exhilarated by his success in this Darwinian trial – and trying not to wheeze too much – Marcello secures his place as Sylvia's escort for the evening. The two urban mountaineers enjoy their shared achievement as Sylvia extols the view in her characteristic bricolage of languages. The scene delights in Rome's newfound glamour – the other side of the coin from Manzù's plaintive reliefs downstairs. It also has some fun with ideas about sexuality and sanctity, Ms Ekberg presenting a somewhat different profile from most Catholic priests. There may also be some pun intended, either a very deep or a very shallow one, on the maternal profile of the dome itself. But what it most straight-forwardly enacts is a narrative of ascent and escape, and the sudden sublimity of finding oneself at the top of St Peter's, wind-blown, gazing – it seems infinitely – outwards.

Even at this stage there are new things to notice. A feature of 29 June, St Peter and St Paul's day, in Rome, used to be the Girandola, a spectacular firework display at the Castel

Sant'Angelo, just along the Tiber from St Peter's. The fire-works were accompanied by lamps lit all over the outside of the basilica. The iron discs where these used to be painstakingly installed by the Sampietrini are still visible, rising in rows up the outside of the dome. The high viewpoint also discloses at last the shape of the church: the way Michelangelo encased his planned Greek cross in diagonal outer walls, buttressing the dome overhead with six thick prisms of masonry; the two big chapels set at the shoulders of the basilica in the late six-teenth century; Maderno's nave; Bernini's piazza; Piacentini's Via Conciliazione and the Castel Sant'Angelo beyond. Of course, from the top of the church you will only be able to see the big picture. But it is quite a picture. A minor pleasure is being able to look down into the Vatican palace and gardens. In a niche at the end of Bramante's courtyard, two long arcaded wings diminishing in height as they run uphill to connect with the Belvedere Villa at the top of the hill, you can make out the Pigna, the huge bronze pinecone which used to stand in the narthex in front of Old St Peter's, and which was fabled to have crowned the Mausoleum of Hadrian, now the Castel Sant'Angelo, in antiquity. The architectural handling of the courtyard gives a taste of what Bramante's St Peter's might have looked like. The sheer untidiness of the site, with buildings tucked into each other at all sorts of angles (some-thing the colonnade disguises rather well from ground level), becomes clear. The forbidding exterior of the Sistine Chapel alongside the north aisle of St Peter's makes a curious con-trast with its jewelled interior. The eccentric appurtenances of a miniature state – a train station, a radio mast – are visible, as well as some of the more interesting buildings in the Vatican, such as Nervi's winglike audience hall on the south side of the basilica, and a couple of churches you would never know were there. You can get some sense of the boundaries of the Vatican, the mighty sixteenth-century fortifications which rise along the western edge of the Vatican hill.

The crown of the dome is also the perfect point from which to observe some of the wider visual dialogues entered into by the basilica. The rough line of domed and cylindrical monuments noticed by the city's cartographers in the sixteenth century, when the unfinished St Peter's won the status of an honorary ruin (see Chapter 3), is plainly visible: from the Pantheon to the Colosseum (what remains of the Amphitheatrum Castrense in the south-eastern corner of the city is harder to make out). Church domes rise from the Campo Marzio, the Tiber's flood-plain, as if thronging to pay tribute to St Peter's: Sant'Andrea della Valle, San Giovanni dei Fiorentini, St Augustine, the Milanese church of San Carlo e Sant' Ambrogio on the Corso, and many others. The blocky mass of the Palazzo Caffarelli, site of the Roman temple of Jupiter, Juno and Minerva, squats on the Capitol hill (now dwarfed by the Vittoriale, the preposterously large, typewriter-shaped monument to Italian unification). The outskirts of Rome are delineated by commercial and industrial development of a kind usually embargoed in the *centro storico*, and by a few newer public buildings – Portoghesi's mosque to the north-west of the city, one dialogue which few in the old Church would have foreseen, and Renzo Piano's Auditorium, a millennial *grand projet* resembling a trio of armadillos at nervous rest. The countryside beyond, and even sometimes the sea to the west, hangs dimly visible in soft washes of colour.

On the southern horizon one can make out Mussolini's

attempt to refound Rome, the Fascist utopia of the Esposizione Universale di Roma or EUR, conceived just before the war and partly completed after it by Piacentini and others. This is dominated by the Palazzo del Cività di Lavoro, a sort of squared-off and pared-down Colosseum. But the Fascist State's new dispensation with the Church is vividly expressed by a Mussolinian riposte to St Peter's, the domed church of St Peter and St Paul. This punctures the skyline south of the city in rather the same way as St Peter's does the north-west. It also bears various similarities to its Vatican counterpart – a framing colonnade, mosaic decoration inside, statues of the Apostles flanking the entrance, and so on – though you won't see much of this from so far away. After the Concordat of 1929, when the Vatican won its extraterritoriality and its privileges, but lost for ever its claim to temporal sovereignty in Italy, such a project could only be understood as a show of strength on the part of the little Caesar who now exercised the earthly power.

Indeed, the most conspicuous feature of the rooftop or dometop view from St Peter's is the long, straight Via della Conciliazione (Fig. 17), and the two pavilions which link it to Bernini's piazza. These are austere classical boxes, cleverly designed to harmonise with the stark architecture of Domenico Fontana's Apostolic Palace, the most imposing part of the Vatican ensemble aside from St Peter's itself. But they are unmistakably Mussolinian as well. They, along with most of the Via Conciliazione, are tenanted by religious organisations, but the arrangement is still manifestly the creation of a secular, authoritarian regime, albeit a creation which pleased the papal authorities immensely. Just as Mussolini literally bulldozed Rome's antique heritage by

17. View from the dome of St Peter's. This view shows the *borghi*, the two medieval streets which used to run eastwards from the Piazza San Pietro, before Mussolini demolished them to make way for the wide, severe Via della Conciliazione.

driving the Via dell'Impero, now the Via dei Fori Imperiali, through the heart of the Forum, so this project was meant to take the tradition of grand urban-planning as carried out by a Julius II or a Sixtus V, and carry it on in the name of the State. Mussolini had himself photographed wielding a pickaxe with manly vigour, clearing away the dusty masonry of old Italy to make way for a new and streamlined Empire. Making the Via Conciliazione entailed demolishing the *borghi*, two crooked medieval streets, and dispersing what left-wing commentators have been quick to point out was a working-class and anti-Fascist neighbourhood. The controversy generated by the project, and the anger felt by some Romans at what seemed to them less like *conciliazione*, reconciliation, than mere horse-trading between the regime and the Church, is best illustrated by paying another visit to Pasquino. When work on the Via Conciliazione resumed after the war, the stubby lamp-posts which ran along it were anonymously denounced as 'suppositories for the Holy Arse', an untranslatable pun on *anno* and *ano*, 1950 being a Jubilee or *Anno Santo*, 'Holy Year'. Many Romans simply could not see why such a tainted scheme was allowed to resume as if nothing had happened, even if they had to concede that the eastern prospect of St Peter's had acquired vastly more grandeur as a result.

There is even a Mussolinian fountain tucked in behind the northern wing of Bernini's colonnade, just next to the *corridoio*, the fortified passage which leads from the Vatican walls to the Castel Sant'Angelo, along which Clement VII fled during the Sack of 1527. The fountain takes the form of a stack of tiaras, piled idly up like bankrupt stock. We've seen plenty of instances of the Popes themselves repackaging their history as heritage, transfiguring the functional into the decorative. This fountain is a good example of the same process – only this time, it isn't the Popes making the point, but their secular successors. The three-crowned tiara was a token of princely power as well as priestly and apostolic status, and so redundant since the loss of the *temporale*, when the burden of *munificentia* passed from the papacy to the State. The fountain is usefully sited on the hot walk from the metro station to Piazza San Pietro; but it is also a nose-thumbing repudiation of the old idea of a Pope of the Romans.

So the view from the top of St Peter's encompasses a lot – spatially, temporally, politically and historically. It is a place from which to think about limits and margins. You feel you are standing at a point from which an obscurely huge range of questions might be settled. In one sense, you are standing at the centre of the world.

To be the centre of the world is to be the object of imitations and representations. Many of the buildings one sees from the crown of St Peter's were influential on it; others influenced by it. Once all exist in the same world it is probably best just to let them carry on their conversation rather than agonise about which came first. Similarly, most visitors to the basilica will already have seen it reflected in other buildings, in Rome or elsewhere, or seen it as if in a picture from some approved viewpoint around the city: from the Vatican gardens, say, or up on the Janiculum or Aventine hills, or by the Quirinal palace, a papal residence until the Risorgimento, or in front of the Villa Medici on the Pincio. Almost certainly they will have seen pictures of the basilica, either close-ups of the façade which are all pomp and circumstance, or more distant views emphasising the dome as a locking-piece on the skyline. This consciousness will inform their perceptions when they eventually find themselves looking back at the place from which they looked before. This is a good metaphor for the visit to the basilica itself: you are here; you look over there; you walk over there; you look back here. Gradually, everything makes a little more sense.

It would be otiose, or at least surplus to requirements, to list all the churches and public buildings which have been influenced by St Peter's, though as we have seen it tells us a lot about St Peter's to know what buildings influenced it. But often imitation is the most banal form of flattery. Old St Peter's was widely used as a template – Durham Cathedral borrows its proportions, for example. There is a church in Bologna (for a long time a papal city) which seems to have been based on the design by Bramante which appeared on a bronze medal in 1506. Another in Naples is purely and simply a scaled-down copy of the basilica as rebuilt, done in cheaper materials and now unhappily marooned next to a motorway junction. A new church in Ivory Coast boasts a dome modelled on, and in fact slightly bigger than, St Peter's. It would be surprising if it were not so. St Peter's, after all, is the mould, template or womb of all churches. In one sense the interesting thing is to note an occasional reluctance to follow the template, as when the newly emancipated British Catholics of the nineteenth century, having flirted with a full-blown Italian Baroque style in the Brompton Oratory, quickly moved on to Gothic or even Byzantine prototypes. Yet the impact of St Peter's has been felt beyond the Catholic world. Church and dome have also exercised influence on Anglican cathedrals, outposts of government, Nazi *folies de grandeur*, an English country house and a shopping mall in Saudi Arabia, to name a few. The consistency of effect which St Peter's largely achieves hasn't stopped it from inspiring diverse and even contradictory imitations.

The most copied elements of St Peter's are the baldacchino and the dome. The Val de Grâce, the former Jesuit church in Paris, elaborates Bernini's four-columned canopy into a dynamic hexagonal arrangement. Many other churches, mostly but not exclusively Catholic, have some variation on the St Peter's theme over their altars. The Solomonic columns used by Bernini, themselves copied from antique prototypes, proliferate in church and domestic architecture, furniture design and – later – cast ironwork. But the case of the dome is more interesting, if only because it is always fairly easy to design a church dome which doesn't look much like St Peter's, so when one encounters one which does one can legitimately suppose that the decision to make it so was a deliberate one.

In church architecture there is a pretty clear consensus about what a dome means. It symbolises the vault of Heaven, and the mystical presence-in-everything of the invisible God. The form of the dome at St Peter's, where a square arrangement of four piers is linked to the circular and hemispherical spaces of drum and dome by what are called pendentives, four concave triangles, is essentially an invention of the Italian Renaissance, even if it draws on Byzantine prototypes to some unguessable degree. The iconography of its mosaics, in which the four Evangelists or gospel-writers mediate between the earthly realm below and the heavenly one above, proceeds from the formal and spatial arrangement logically enough (at any rate, such iconography is widely used, in Orthodox as well as Catholic churches). The idea of a dome-shaped void which means something abstract and infinite can easily be applied to other types of religious and secular architecture – and the uses of a large dome as a focal point in an urban design, a mystical union of vertical and horizontal elements, are manifest. So we shouldn't be too surprised at how wide-ranging the impact of St Peter's has been.

Nevertheless, some imitations of the basilica have the power to raise an eyebrow. It comes as no surprise at all to find ribbed domes or baldacchinos on Catholic churches built in Europe and beyond during the seventeenth and eight-eenth centuries. The architectural tribute precisely mirrors the tributary cultural and power structures of the Church itself during the period. Less inevitable is the fact that several Protestant states and statelets borrow extensively from St Peter's during the same period. In Protestant Germany, in Denmark, even in England, churches adopt elements from St Peter's, principally the dome, but other things as well, and try to naturalise or tame them. The lovely Fredrikskirke in Amelienborg, Copenhagen, built by Nicolai Eigtved in the mid-eighteenth century, is a round, domed church with a richness of exterior detail and a heavy, slightly elliptical dome on top. Its interior is stark and unadorned, with nothing of the polychromy or decorative animation of St Peter's. Sir Christopher Wren's designs for St Paul's Cathedral in London went through some half a dozen distinct revisions between the fire of 1666 and the 1690s, when work began in earnest. All of them contained some explicit reference to St Peter's, usually in the treatment of the dome. Yet the church as built diverges from St Peter's more significantly than any of its previous avatars. The dome of St Paul's resembles an overgrown version of Bramante's Tempietto (see Chapter 3). This is a decisive shift from the so-called Penultimate design, in which the main dome is a dead ringer for St Peter's and the two smaller towers over the west end echo the Tempietto. Wren went beyond Michelangelo and his assistants in segregating his inner dome from his outer by means of a third structure, a cone of brick, with the result that the outside of St Paul's bears surprisingly little relation to the inside. Later designs for St Paul's also part company with St Peter's in having a two-storey elevation wrapped round the outside of the building instead of Michelangelo's giant pilasters and heavy attic. Many art historians have noticed that the form of the cathedral follows an English medieval template of a long, lowish nave and chancel rather than the hybrid but emphatically vertical interior space of St Peter's. St Paul's is even vaulted by a series of domes rather than a single barrel-vault (these are held up by little flying buttresses, another medieval device).

All in all, there is plenty of evidence that Wren wanted to show his knowledge of Italian church architecture, both Renaissance and contemporary (among other things), but that he and his patrons the Dean and Chapter of St Paul's did not want a building which would bend the knee to St Peter's too readily. Their reasons for this are obvious, and more religious than aesthetic. It was an inconvenience, to put it no higher, that Catholic, absolutist Italy was such a potent cultural lodestar for the Protestant powers of northern Europe, and the manoeuvres which their artists performed to ensure that they did not merely imitate Italian models passively, but sought to incorporate some active transformation into the process, recall precisely and ironically the exertions of Italian sixteenth- and seventeenth-century designers to absorb the lessons of classical antiquity without being overwhelmed by its hefty legacy. Similar triangulations are in evidence in a later church, the Orthodox cathedral of St Isaac in St Petersburg, designed by Auguste de Montferrand in the mid-nineteenth century. Here a dome modelled on St Paul's caps a church with four gigantic porticoes evocative of the Pantheon, and an interior decorated with fetishistically detailed mosaics and lavish coloured marbles in the St Peter's manner. The church asserts itself in the face of its models by means of sheer material ostentation; the marbles speak loudly and clearly of Russia's mineral wealth, as does the thick mercury-gilding on the outside of the dome.

Predictably enough, secular buildings modelled on St Peter's handle its influence still more nervously. The symbolism of the dome was so imprecise that it could easily be made to express secular qualities, civic or judicial, instead of religious ones. Its geometrical perfection might even make it a useful emblem of Reason, a faculty which has often been said to be the very antipathy of religious belief. Yet the best-known domes came from religious buildings, and so imitating them in secular ones was a task of some delicacy. The Founding Fathers of the United States of America held attitudes to their European predecessors which were ambivalent at best. Deists or nonconformists themselves, they disliked the notion of centralised, established religion exemplified by the Catholic Church. Yet the notion of the city on a hill is drenched in Christian symbolism, and the secularism which commentators have often seen as the best guarantee of civil rights in America is nowadays looking pretty flimsy (that line about 'one nation under God' tends to give the game away). Nevertheless, in formally separating Church and State the Americans went beyond what had been attempted in Europe to date. Their decision early in the nineteenth century to incorporate a simplified copy of the dome of St Peter's into their national seat of government therefore comes as something of a surprise. The architects of the Capitol, from Benjamin Latrobe to Thomas Walter, were skilled practitioners of a pared-down neoclassicism lately fashionable in France. In adopting St Peter's as a model while purging it of its 'excesses' of ornament, as Walter did when he rebuilt Latrobe's rather Pantheon-ish dome in the mid-nineteenth century, he was acting out the prejudices of neoclassical critics like Milizia. He was also exploiting the power of a large dome to give concrete expression to abstract ideas. A big enough and harmonious enough space might speak of the nobility of good government as eloquently as of any species of Deity. In fact, it might speak so eloquently that the niceties of the message were drowned out by the sublimity of the medium.

This brings us to what must be the most notorious of St Peter's stepchildren across the world. During the 1930s, Albert Speer helped Hitler design Germania, the bloated megalopolis which was to replace Berlin after Nazi Germany's inevitable forthcoming triumph. Germania was a prime specimen of the 'statolatry' against which both Pius XI and XII spoke out. It was also a good example of how a strain of German Romantic thought, intensively preoccupied with the idea of Italy, was both assimilated and perverted by the Nazis. Giving your dream city a Latin name rather than a German one might seem like an odd thing for a fanatically nationalistic dictator to do. But the Nazis made free with history like children with a dressing-up box. As well as Norse myth, medieval chivalry, a peculiar interest in Catharism and so on, they had a deep thing about Rome. On his 1939 visit there Hitler even followed the route taken by the victorious Charles V of Habsburg four centuries before (though Charles was Flemish by birth, and said he only spoke German to his horse). The idea that the Germans had withstood and even sometimes defeated the ancient Romans was a source of mild embarrassment to classically educated intellectuals of the *Goethezeit*. But to men of a more practical outlook, the key thing was that Charlemagne, who revived and perpetuated the Empire, was some kind of a German as well. Germania would represent many things: an imperial capital (its Latin name a token of its international prestige), a revived Rome, a concrete manifestation of the 1,000-year Reich. It is characteristic of Hitler's intense, almost necrophiliac political morbidity that he commissioned drawings of Germania in ruins to see whether they would live up to those left by ancient civilisations.

The recollections of St Peter's in Speer's designs for the Great Hall in Germania are not entirely undisguised. As with the Washington Capitol, the dome is streamlined and simplified – it is also inflated to an almost unbuildable scale. Unusually, there is more or less nothing beneath the dome, just a single low storey, with a long portico on the south side – a primitive simplicity of form which had been handed down to Speer from some of the wilder French neoclassicists at the turn of the nineteenth century. The building seems to sit on the ground like a handbell (in this it resembles the new Cathedral of Our Lady in Ivory Coast, where the dome is much more like St Peter's, but has little or no church underneath it). The hall forms a part of a monumental avenue punctuated with arches and columns, a Nazi Champs-Elysées. Nothing of Bernini's empathetic approach to monumental urban space can be discerned, though there are parallels with the urbanism of Sixtus V in the late sixteenth century, which proved so influential on the France of Louis XIV and other *anciens régimes* thereafter.

The stark giganticism of Germania is a perfect example of how the twentieth-century dictatorships hijacked Enlightenment ideas about rationalising public life. In Italy, Piacentini wrote that 'the greatest and most beautiful monuments of Rome are hidden in holes. In one hole is St Peter's, in another the Trevi Fountain, in another the Pantheon. Paris, Berlin, London, Brussels: all created almost from scratch in the nineteenth century.' In other words, driving straight, wide streets all over the city was a simple matter of progress and clarity. He even talked about moving a famous public telescope from the Calle Aragno to the dome of St Peter's, making the building a new kind of Panopticon. Piacentini wasn't without his critics. One leading academic opposed 'this fever to see all of Rome from a single point ... let's just build a revolving platform in Piazza Venezia for tourists in a hurry!' Yet in reality the urbanism which Piacentini and his colleagues devised for Mussolini followed just the same trajectory as Speer's more overtly triumphalist plans: to overwhelm; to make the human being feel small and fragile; to express State power in terms of eternity and infinity – in short, to adapt the notion of the sublime to political events.

Sublimity, according to Burke, is when 'the mind is so entirely filled with its object that it cannot entertain any other'. Kant said something slightly different: the 'mathematic' sublime was 'that which is not to be sought in nature, but only in our ideas', while the 'dynamic' sublime was 'that which is felt when we observe in nature mighty objects from which we are in no danger, and regard these objects as fearful without being afraid of them'. Both writers moved on somewhat from classical notions of the sublime; for Longinus, it was simply 'a certain distinction and excellence in expression', whose effect was 'not persuasion but transport'.

During the eighteenth century notions of sublimity came to be an important part of the conventional language used to describe one's responses to certain kinds of art. St Peter's was a case in point. Eighteenth-century Grand Tourists were much exercised by the question of whether it looked smaller than it actually was, as though to look its actual size would be some sort of shattering abomination (this is still a commonplace in many tourist guidebooks; even in this book I've repeatedly found myself returning to questions of scale, and the visitor's consciousness of it). If the church looked smaller than it was, that might be a tribute to its elegance of design, or a regrettable want of sublimity according to taste. In any case, the never less than estimable size of the basilica might be hoped to induce an authentic frisson of sublimity – though what constituted the sensation was purposely left vague, except that it was some admixture of aesthetic appreciation, apprehension and an almost erotic sense of desire. The feeling of being violently confronted by one's own subjectivity might sound like a good one to avoid. But broadly, during the late eighteenth century, sublimity was regarded as more and more of a good thing, as if more and more people had tried a rollercoaster for the first time and found they liked it. Going into a vast church like St Peter's was curiously seen as a little like contemplating a ruin of unimaginable antiquity, or even crossing a perilous Alpine pass.

To the age of Sensibility, an extreme manifestation of which an appreciation of the sublime arguably was, St Peter's impact on the emotions was more important than its status as an object lesson in architectural or ecclesiastical history – an odd reprise of the Counter-Reformation's insistence on a sensual and even visceral approach to worship. Madame de Staël's *Corinne* takes us into the basilica during Holy Week, when a candlelit cross is the only light inside (this ought to be wrong, since the lamps ringing the *confessio* are said to remain constantly lit. Indeed the shrine of St Peter has purportedly been lamp-lit since antiquity, when olives were grown on the Vatican hill to provide oil for the purpose). 'The living …' she says, 'seem like pygmies compared with the images of the dead.' A shorthand version of a broadly similar response can be found in the travel journals of James Boswell, generally less preoccupied with articulating his aesthetic experiences than recounting his amatory ones: '… went to St Peter's. Approached grand area, piazza &c. Not struck enough, but increased. Entered church; warm. Ah! noble, immense, quite rapt.'

The extent to which spiritual dimensions entered into all this is highly questionable. It could be argued that the sublime was merely a displacement or reconfiguration of waning religious sensibilities. But the specific religious character of St Peter's was anyway nothing if not problematic. British Grand Tourists were by no means all Protestant

– Charles Townley, one of the most important collectors of antiquities in the eighteenth century, was a Catholic peer barred by his religion from Parliament, for example – but as we've seen, religious distinctions were elaborately intertwined with political ones. Seeing and judging a church – especially St Peter's – as a work of art tended to diminish its power to stir up broader anxieties. Yet even travellers or connoisseurs from Catholic countries might see some lessening of ancient religious or expressive powers in such a building. Victor Hugo devotes a chapter of *Notre-Dame de Paris* to the history of architecture. Beginning with a remark made by the Gothic church's archdeacon Claude Frollo, *le livre tuera l'édifice* or 'the book will kill the building', he identifies the invention of the printed book in the fifteenth century as the start of a long decline in the eloquence of architecture. St Peter's is cited as, in effect, the last great building; its many imitations are '… a mania … a pity'. Hugo exploits the biblical pun on 'Peter' and 'stone': *Saint-Pierre* means 'holy stone' as well as 'St Peter's'. His solemn melancholy is not so far in its purpose from Stendhal's acid wit. Post-Enlightenment society has lost the gift of wonder. What is more – and here he parts company from Stendhal, though he anticipates the Gothic Revivalism of Ruskin and Pugin in England – it will not find it again by looking back to classical antiquity or the Renaissance, but rather in the crepuscular Middle Ages.

Happily, stout commonsense and proportion tend to prevail over the tremulous gloom of sublimity in most travellers' accounts of St Peter's. Henry James, an acute commentator on Italy even if his travel writing was mostly done to keep the pot boiling, sees in St Peter's a cheerful, matter-of fact quality. He notes that in it light 'performs the office of gloom and mystery in Gothic churches', and writes that it 'speaks less of aspiration than of full and convenient assurance'. Set against the artistic absolutism of the basilica, its many claims to uniqueness, its power to overwhelm, is a constant instinct to inquire, measure and compare. Lassels's manuscript *Description of Italy*, written to advise a Catholic peer in the mid-seventeenth century, then later published as the *Italian Voyage*, strikes an early note of prosaic reasonableness. 'Coming therefore near to St Peter's Church, I was glad to see that noble structure where greatness and neatness, bulk and beauty, are so mingled together, that it's neither neat only, like a spruce Gallery; nor vast only, like a great Hall; but it's rather like a proper man, and yet well proportioned.' Even when he dutifully acknowledges the exceptional qualities of St Peter's he does so in an implicitly comparative framework: 'It hath put all Antiquity to the Blush, and all Posterity to the non-plus.'

In 1705, Joseph Addison had something characteristically level-headed to say about the size issue: 'It seems neither extremely high, nor long, nor broad, because it is all of 'em in a just Equality.' In other ways, Addison was bitterly critical of Italy, noting that 'There is not a more miserable people in Italy than the Pope's subjects', decrying the 'Swarms of Vagabonds under the title of Pilgrims' and complaining that 'Young & lusty Beggars ... consume the Charity that ought to support the Sickly, Old and Decrepit.' The notion that Italy was a land in terminal decline, and that visiting even modern Italian monuments was like going to an archaeological site, became axiomatic among visitors from more prosperous regions. Northall's popular *Travels through Italy* of 1766 even opens with the line, 'What Egypt was to the antients

Italy is to the moderns.' This attitude made the expropriation of art works and antiquities from impoverished Italian
nobles at knock-down prices seem less like gangsterism and
more like good cultural husbandry. It also enabled visitors to
St Peter's to see it as belonging to the past rather than the
present, even though little nips and tucks to the fabric continued throughout the eighteenth century and beyond. Rather
than the flagship of a living, breathing religious organisation,
it was an honorary ruin – only in a rather different sense from
that understood by the artists who had sketched it under construction in the sixteenth century, or engraved it into maps
of Rome in the same state. This was a ruin whose physical state was miraculously preserved (and there's no evidence
that eighteenth-century visitors found St Peter's in any way
dilapidated, as they found Venice, say), but whose founding
civilisation had evaporated as surely as Rome or Byzantium.
Needless to say, this antiquarian reading of the basilica also
enabled Protestant tourists to sidestep the troublesome issue
of religion (just as religious art tended to be discussed in
purely aesthetic terms).

On this reading, attempts to judge St Peter's by compar-
ing it to other buildings need not be settled in the former's
favour. Around the turn of the nineteenth century, John
Moore wrote that the façade of St Peter's was 'inferior to
our St Paul's'. In his Royal Academy lectures of a few years
before, the great neoclassical architect Sir John Soane was
keen to keep St Peter's in proportion, or rather, dispropor-
tion, confirming that it looked smaller than it was, and that
this was in some sense a defect. The doors were too small,
the statues too big. Maderno was 'that patronised block-
head, that selfcreated architect'. Soane also pronounced St

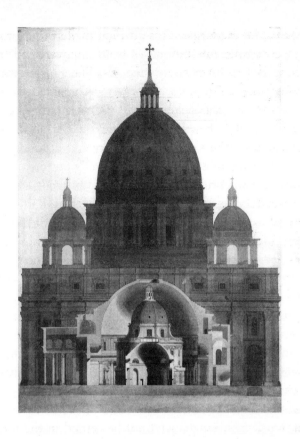

18. Comparative illustration showing St Peter's, the Pantheon, the Radcliffe Observatory, Oxford and the Bank of England in London, by Sir John Soane. Soane's architectural teaching relied heavily on these comparative images. Here St Peter's presides over a 'family' of domed structures, the smallest of which, designed by Soane himself, may perhaps be read as 'correcting' some of the errors of its more imposing predecessors. The Pantheon, as formally perfect as it was almost universally felt to be, has an attribute common in Roman monumental architecture, namely 'redundancy': the walls are thicker than they need to be to hold up the dome. Arguably, the resulting sense of mass is part of the building's appeal, though neoclassical purists didn't always see things that way.

Peter's inferior to St Paul's from the outside (though superior from the inside). Meanwhile, 'Although the magnificence and richness of Catholic churches cannot be exceeded, it is painful to trace a tiresome and unaccountable monotony in the architecture of so many of these religious structures.' This echoes a comment by Sir William Chambers, a generation older than Soane, and a much more orthodox classicist in his own work: 'St Peter's at Rome offers ten thousand colours to the sight, which divide the attention by confusing the form.' Both architects display the intellectual's distrust of the sensual – not to mention the Protestant's distrust of the Catholic.

As an architectural educator, Soane was preoccupied with canons, lists of comparable works which could buttress students' sense of history, and guide their artistic values. In an age before slide-projectors and PowerPoint presentations, he made surprisingly extensive use of visual material in his lectures. Large drawings in watercolour and gouache were made by Soane, his assistant Joseph Gandy and his students, then pinned up around the lecture-hall for students to examine on Soane's cue. One distinctive, not to say pioneering, type of drawing was the comparative elevation or section, in which similar buildings were depicted next to or nestling inside one another.

Two of these feature St Peter's. One shows it looming over a little family of domed buildings (Fig. 18): the Pantheon, rendered in section like a sliced fruit; James Gibbs's Radcliffe Library or Camera in Oxford, and Soane's own Dividend Office from the Bank of England in the City of London. The resulting dense montage brings us back to those indigestible Roman delicacies mentioned in Chapter 3. This way of representing buildings allowed for exact comparisons of scale and detailing, and, in the sliced areas, for some hints to be dropped about structure (the thickness of the lower part of the Pantheon's dome, for example). It also suggested a filiation between buildings of a similar form or born of the same tradition. What is striking about this drawing (as opposed to the other one, which shows a more conventional face-off between St Peter's in Rome and St Paul's in London) is that the functions of all four buildings are very different. The image is an essay in the dome as theme and variations. Its alternating sections and elevations lend it an almost Baroque sense of delight in the interplay of closed or convex forms and open or concave ones (Soane's critical opinion of Bernini notwithstanding). It plays around with the most obvious hierarchy one might impose on this particular set of buildings, that of size – the Pantheon's dome is slightly wider than that of St Peter's – though you wouldn't know that from the picture – and instead draws our attention to qualitative criteria of proportion and construction. The eminence of St Peter's is subtly challenged by the formal purity of the Pantheon, the intricate rhythms of Gibbs's building and the stark delicacy of Soane's Bank, where the dome is a terracotta honeycomb and a fairy ring of Greek caryatids is the only relief from the architect's characteristic minimalism. Just as in previous centuries the moderns could surpass the ancients through richness of decoration, variety of invention or sheer enormity, so the moderns of the present, neoclassical age could hold their creations up proudly against the achievements of their predecessors, both Renaissance and antique, on the basis of elegance of proportion, ingenuity of structure or correctness of ornament.

Soane's cutaway suggests a dissection of St Peter's and the

three smaller domes inside it, an urge to measure, tabulate and compare. It is a world away from the many works of art which have shown the dome breaking the Roman skyline, bridging heaven and earth, forming a spatial and temporal fulcrum in this most multidimensional of cities. The last duty of the visitor who would truly get the measure of St Peter's is to step away from it and try to see it from the back, either by taking the garden tour, or walking up around the fortifications or climbing the Janiculum to the south. The dome makes much more sense when seen above Michelangelo's powerful, sculptural walls than when diffidently peering over the nave and façade on the eastern side. The giant pilasters bunched up like sinews, the snarling windows (whether or not these were what Michelangelo intended) in the heavy attic, the sense of compactness even on such a large scale – all add up to achieve an almost expressionistic effect analogous to the squeezed rectangle of the Piazza del Campidoglio (see Chapter 1).

From further afield the impact of the church is inevitably less strong, but still distinctive. A nineteenth-century print shows St Peter's from a popular viewpoint just in front of the Villa Medici, on the Pincio near the top of the Spanish Steps (Fig. 19). The villa passed to France as part of Maria de'Medici's dowry when she married Henry IV; later, it became an outpost of the French Academy, a purpose it still serves today. French artists from Claude to Corot have stepped outside the villa to draw or paint the mighty basilica cresting the horizon, though their standpoint is now a little overgrown by trees. My print shows the heavy marble fountain framing Michelangelo's dome like a saucer beneath an upended teacup. It also displays a very nineteenth-century

19. St Peter's from the Pincio, anonymous engraving, late nineteenth century. This is one of the most famous views of St Peter's. The trees are bigger now, but the view still exists. Even better is the view from the bar in the Villa Medici, above and behind the terrace depicted here.

preoccupation with local colour: a small cohort of doleful priests, and a solitary Roman matron in traditional dress with a basket of grapes improbably perched on her head are artfully disposed around the terrace to give movement and authenticity. The dome is just a silhouette, pale and faint, hovering in the distant haze, just as in reality the heat and smog of Rome can flatten out details and cushion the impact of even the most imposing monument. There would seem to be little point in thinking about ideas of sublimity here. But as calmed as the impact of St Peter's is by dust and distance, it is still rendered by the printmaker (who in this respect is following the precedent laid down by his more illustrious colleagues) as the only building of any size or character in the city, which is certainly not true. The approach is not unlike some of the antiquarian prints of Giovanni Battista Piranesi, who imagined the Campo Marzio purged of all but its ancient Roman buildings, as if Rome were a desert city reclaimed by nothingness after its fall.

These distant apparitions of the dome of St Peter's, hovering on the horizon like a mirage, provide the final key to understanding the building. Even several miles from the Aurelian walls encircling old Rome, lolling in the scrawny parkland beside the Via Appia Pignatelli, surrounded by grazing sheep and ruined Roman tombs, one can't escape the dome. It presides over an entire city, and more than 2,000 years of its history. The most remarkable thing about St Peter's is simply that it *abides*. Its shape has changed over the centuries, and its use and meaning scarcely less so. Few tourists today perceive its rich and contentious relationship with antiquity. Few pilgrims have much interest in the sort of Catholicism it was rebuilt to express. But it continues to be the *matrice* of the Codex Chigi, to send its progeny out into the world, to Africa, Asia and America; to generate new interpretations and to serve its different constituencies in new ways. As an architectural and ecclesiastical archetype, a flawed, perfect building, it reverberates still.

FURTHER READING

The following is not meant as any kind of exhaustive bibliography, but rather as a series of modest proposals for readers who would like to think about the building in more depth than I have been able to treat it. It is also meant to signal my gratitude to authors who have been especially helpful to me.

GENERAL

The most thorough general guide to the basilica in English is by James Lees-Milne (*St Peter's*, 1967). It has a straightforward linear structure, and offers several brisk pen-portraits of popes and artists. Some statements about the archaeology of the building have been contradicted by more recent work. A faint odour of sanctity hangs over the enterprise; the book so pleased the papal authorities that Lees-Milne was invited to join a Committee of Honour which was to examine the Cathedra Petri and pronounce on its authenticity. While up on the scaffold scrutinising the relic, Lees-Milne saw that the statues flanking Bernini's colossal bronze reliquary were unfinished on the westward side, from which they were not ordinarily visible. He records his disappointment in his diary: 'I had expected them to have hollow insides, but not to lack backsides, so to speak.'

Another good general and practical account can be found on a website, www.stpetersbasilica.org, an extensive and companionable medley of blogs, book extracts, press photographs and archaeological diagrams. Lees-Milne's book is posted almost wholesale under the heading, *The History*. The site proclaims its independence from the Vatican, but is emphatically *parti pris* – the entry on Canova's Stuart monument calls the Prince Regent 'the Hereditary Prince of Hanover', for example. The Italian culture ministry, in cahoots with the Fabbrica di San Pietro, has produced an outstanding guide to St Peter's in its *Roma Sacra* series, though the text has that windy quality which translation from a Romance language into a Germanic one tends to bring.

ART HISTORY

Art-historical writing on the basilica can be offputtingly austere, and is often both confused and confusing. Much of it hinges on attempts to attribute a large stack of Renaissance drawings now in the Uffizi in Florence, though scholars have tried to date work on the rebuilding of the church by various other means, one article attempting to analyse payments made to the mule-drovers who carried spoil from the site during Michelangelo's stint as architect. The most thorough book is also the latest to appear in English, *St Peter's in the Vatican*, ed. William Tronzo (2005). Especially interesting is Dale Kinney's chapter on *spolia*, reused antique materials, in the early Christian Church. James Ackerman's books on Michelangelo and Howard Hibbard's short monograph on Bernini (1965) are meaty without being too obscure. There is currently not much in English on Bramante. Vasari's *Lives of the Most Excellent Painters, Sculptors and Architects* (2nd expanded edition, 1568) is currently available in various English translations, all abridged. Condivi's *Life of Michelangelo* exists in a good 1999 English version by Alice Sedgwick Wohl. Bernini's son Domenico wrote an endearing and affectionate biography of his father, but it seems never to have been rendered into English. An exciting, laudable and partly successful attempt to eke an entire book out of the fabled conflict between Bernini and Boromini is *The Genius in the Design: Bernini, Borromini and the Rivalry that Transformed Rome* by Jake Morrissey (2005). A crucial episode in Morrissey's story is the collapse of Bernini's bell-tower; Sarah McPhee's *Bernini and the Bell-towers: Architecture and Politics at the Vatican* (2002) submits that incident to an impressively close analysis. A good book on the urban context of the basilica from Bernini to Mussolini is Leonardo Benevolo's *San Pietro e la città di Roma* (2004). *Piazza San Pietro* by Birindelli (1981) and Borsi's 1980 *Bernini Architetto* are also excellent.

For the theoretical background to the earliest initiatives to rebuild the basilica, Rudolf Wittkower's *Architectural Principles in the Age of Humanism* (revised edition, 1988) still takes some beating, though there has been something of a backlash against his ideas over the past decade or so. Other theoretical books which have helped me enormously include various works by Gottfried Semper, the most deep-thinking architectural theorist of the nineteenth century.

ANCIENT HISTORY AND LITERATURE

Where possible I used the Loeb editions of ancient authors,

seduced by their parallel English and Latin/Greek versions, not to mention their generally excellent commentaries. Sorcha Carey's work on Pliny was illuminating. I read some article literature on Early Christian burial ritual, and a few extracts from the *Liber Pontificalis* and various martyrologies in poetry and prose, but I wouldn't necessarily recommend them to the casual reader. More enlightening was *Death, Burial and Rebirth in the Religions of Antiquity* by Jon Davies (1999), which underlined for me the untidy fusion of belief-systems which existed in the ancient world.

OLD ST PETER'S AND THE VATICAN NECROPOLIS

Fr Niggl's lavish 1972 edition of the so-called Grimaldi MS provides a full visual record of the tombs and mosaics as they stood in the surviving eastern half of Constantine's basilica just before its final demolition. My understanding of the porphyry *rota* was enhanced by Philippe Malgouyres's unexpectedly gripping Louvre exhibition catalogue *Porphyre: La Pierre Pourpre des Ptolemées à Bonaparte* (2003). Among books about the Roman and Early Christian necropolis under the Grottoes, I enjoyed John Evangelist Walsh's *The Bones of St Peter* (1983), which may take the party line on the authenticity of the remains beneath the high altar of the basilica, but which leaves the reader in no doubt as to what a shambles the excavation and authentication processes were. Toynbee and Ward-Perkins's *The Shrine of St Peter and the Vatican Excavations* (1956) gives a more thorough, though not more critical, account. The Vatican does a charmingly out-of-date guide, but only in Italian – it's on sale in the Ufficio Scavi beside the church. Two articles by J. M. Huskinson and

Philip Fehl made two strong cases for two different sites of Peter's martyrdom.

GENERAL/BACKGROUND HISTORY

I read Cyril Mango's *Byzantium: the Empire of the New Rome* (1980), and – bits of – Gibbon's *Decline and Fall of the Roman Empire*, which may be heroically inaccurate as history but is at least a model of one sort of English prose, and exemplifies one way of thinking about both antiquity and Christianity (Everyman 2-vol. edition, 1993). I read odds and ends on Charlemagne; especially illuminating was a collection of essays ambitiously entitled *The Coronation of Charlemagne: What Did It Signify?* ed. R. E. Sullivan (1959), but also useful was *The Holy Roman Empire: a Dictionary Handbook*, ed. Zophy (1980). A series of books on papal ritual by Agostino Paravicini-Bagliani was both instructive and absorbing, especially *Le chiave e la tiara: immagini e simboli del papato medioevale* (1998).

In This Most Perfect Paradise by Carroll Westfall (1974) deals with Nicholas V, the prototypical builder Pope, in some detail. Richard Krautheimer's *The Rome of Alexander VII 1655–1667* (1985) is excellent. For eighteenth-century Rome and the cult of ruins, see John Wilton-Ely's *The Mind and Art of Giovanni Battista Piranesi* (1978), which contains good reproductions of all Piranesi's Roman views. A sound (if *slightly* arch) appreciation of the cultural significance of ruins is *In Ruins* by Christopher Woodward (2001).

Denis Mack Smith's *Italy: A Modern History* (1959) is still indispensable, as is his *The Making of Italy 1796–1866* (1968). The Longman History of the Papacy is still in a fledgling state, but A. D. Wright's *The Early Modern Papacy: from the Council of Trent to the French Revolution* (2000) helped me a great deal. *Papal Heraldry* by D. L. Galbreath, ed. G. Briggs (1972) helped me decipher the crests which infest Rome. The best English-speaking (though Italian-born) papal historian is Lord Acton, of 'absolute power corrupts absolutely' fame. General editions of his work seem thin on the ground, though one representative cross-section is *Essays in the Liberal Interpretation of History*, ed. MacNeill (1967). As a jobbing WEA lecturer I was delighted to learn that some of Acton's most brilliant work was delivered in a draughty church hall in Bridgnorth, Shropshire.

A bracingly outraged inquest into Mussolini's reworking of Rome is *Mussolini urbanista: lo sventramento* [disembowelling] *di Roma negli anni del consenso* by Antonio Cederna (1980). There is now a tourist guide to EUR. For a thumbnail sketch of the Catholic Church from the Second Vatican Council to the present I went to Rupert Shortt's characteristically clearsighted biography of Benedict XVI, *Commander of the Faith* (2005). On a less elevated plane I have benefited enormously from a number of popular books on the papacy, among the most recent of which was a two-volume set, *I Papi: Storia e Segreti*, by the formidably prolific Claudio Rendina. Even if such books don't necessarily carry enormous scholarly weight, they provide the foreigner and non-Catholic with valuable glimpses of the way in which Italians perceive what they continue to regard to some extent as their one remaining global franchise. They are also very good for pasquinades and reproductions of popular prints, newspaper cartoons and the like.

The most conspicuous literary tribute to St Peter's, and to the enduring mystique of the papacy, must presently be Dan Brown's *Angels and Demons* (2001). It is hard to know what to say about the book; readers who don't already know it must by now be a tiny, embattled minority. It is a breathy thriller in which a 'symbologist' – not a symbolist or symbolologist, note – thwarts a dastardly attempt by the Illuminati, whoever they may be, to detonate a small but lethal quantity of antimatter, whatever that may be, somewhere in the Vatican during a difficult conclave. As a Victorian theatregoer observed while watching the death-throws of Cleopatra: how very different from home life of our own dear Queen.

A less well-known novel about the papacy deserves to be rescued from its present near-oblivion and feted as a minor classic, or even enthroned as the masterpiece in a genre of one. *Hadrian the Seventh* by F. R. Rolfe, an itinerant pederast who sometimes went under the name of Baron Corvo, is an autobiographical fantasy from 1904 (various editions). Its narrator experiences the same deluge of misfortunes as its author – drummed out of the seminary, dogged by poverty and scandal thereafter – but is rescued and vindicated when he finds himself elected Pope. He promptly whitewashes his apartments, sells off all the Vatican's art treasures (here we see an early instance of that ascetic strain of Catholicism which would become so prevalent in the twentieth century) and fires off a series of plain-speaking Epistles to the Great Powers of Europe, before falling prey to an assassin's bullet. Corvo's historical sense was pedantically detailed – I have nowhere come across a fuller description of the elaborate rituals of the pre-1958 conclave, for example – while his prose style was described by one admirer, quoted in A. J. A. Symons's remarkable 1934 biography *The Quest of Corvo*, as 'tyrianthine', the word 'purple' being, apparently, not purple enough.

Some travel guides are as good as an art history book, for example the Blue Guide to Rome by Alta Macadam (2000). Best practical guide to the classical city is the *Oxford Archaeological Guide to Rome* (1998), which, however, omits to say much about Early Christian structures even when these are adjacent to or even mingled with pagan Roman structures of only a few years before. James Boswell's Grand Tour journals (various editions) are predictably racy, even if they don't say much about art and architecture. Various editions of Smollett, Addison and Sterne exist. Recent academic studies of eighteenth-century travel tend to be rather dour. Among more recent travellers Henry James, Charles Dickens and Sigmund Freud are all worth reading on Rome.

I have deliberately tried to make this book a sort of Frankenstein's monster in which elements of cultural and political history, architectural criticism, travel writing, etc. combine and lurch into life. There aren't too many parallels for such an approach. I have enjoyed looking at popular 'microhistories', and at the 'speed history' practised by pamphleteers marching under the banner of the London Psychogeographical Association in the 1970s and 80s – and I've noticed the profitable dilution of their techniques in works by Iain Sinclair and Peter Ackroyd. Such writers – and their forebears in the Situationist International and elsewhere – have helped me think about walking, space, identity and power; and many others – I'd single out Benjamin, Borges, Chatwin, Proust and Sebald – about architecture and memory. Gilles Deleuze's *The Fold: Leibniz and the Baroque*

(1992) is pretty dense, but powerfully original on the way historical and architectural space have been mapped or modelled.

Pictures which represent St Peter's as a marker on the Roman skyline, or as an emblem of the city, are multitudinous. Increasingly, museums and galleries are making their collections available to view on the internet, but don't bank on it. The British Museum and the V&A will both have copies of the best-known prints by Piranesi and Vasi in the eighteenth century (there's a wonderful collection of Claude drawings in the BM too, including his *liber veritatis*). Corot's sketchy painting of St Peter's from the Pincio is in the Hugh Lane Gallery, Dublin.

La Dolce Vita, Roma: Città Aperta, Accatonel, L'Avventura and Fellini's Rome movies all come up from time to time on the art-house cinema circuit, and all seem available on DVD. Charismatic film stills may be available for download – try emailing immaginicinema@inwind.it, or go to www.cinecitta.com.

PLANNING A VISIT?

St Peter's is one of relatively few churches in Rome not to close for a long lunch (the Pantheon is another). Its usual opening hours are 7 a.m.–7 p.m., though during Holy Week, Epiphany, Christmas, etc. access may be restricted (and traffic may be heavy). If you want to see the Pope in action, check the Vatican's website, www.vatican.va. Sunday at noon seems a safe bet for a papal apparition at, and a blessing from, the second window from the right in the Apostolic Palace, which is the large boxy building ahead of you and to your right if you stand near the obelisk in Piazza San Pietro looking towards the basilica. Appearances within the basilica are rarer and more unpredictable, though Holy Week, Christmas and St Peter and St Paul's day (29 June) are likely. Papal audiences can be arranged in advance – check the website for details.

For the Grottoes, you join what is often a long queue outside the basilica to the north side of the façade, then snake sclerotically under the arch sustaining the Pauline chapel, along the north wall of the nave between the basilica and the Vatican palace, down one of the staircases set into the outside wall of the building, and round a prearranged and roped-off route. A dedicated entrance has been built near the arch but isn't yet in use as I write this.

To visit the Necropolis, book well in advance (tel. +39 06

6987 3017 or email uff.scavi@fsp.va). A new necropolis, or a different part of the existing one, has been excavated under one of the car parks near the basilica, but has not yielded any prestigious remains to date. It is, however, also visitable if you book ahead. To visit the gardens, fax in advance to +39 06 6988 5100 or ask in the ticket office to the left of the basilica steps.

To climb the roof go through the arch on the north side of the façade. Be careful not to join the queue for the Grottoes by mistake, unless you want to do that too. The climb is strenuous (323 steps), but there is a small cash saving if you don't take the lift. Bear in mind that the lift only gets you as far as the roof, so the most cramped and difficult part of the climb, the ascent of the dome, is ineluctable. But the roof is worth going up to in any case.

It is quite a slog to get round the Vatican museums, especially if you want to see St Peter's on the same day. The entrance is in Viale Vaticano, near Ottaviano-San Pietro metro station. A one-way system is in operation, and the crowds can be oppressive. Usual cost is 12 euros, though it's free on the last Sunday of every month (it's closed on other Sundays). But there is a lot in the Vatican which can enhance one's impressions of the basilica, even if the two structures only touch clumsily at the north end of St Peter's façade (and secretly at the level of the Grottoes, where there's a passage from church to palace).

The museums proper have a pronounced secular slant, no doubt reflecting the roots of papal collecting in Renaissance humanism. Julius II's inscription on the entrance to the Belvedere villa, the original epicentre of the museums, quoted Virgil: *procul iste profani* or 'keep away you unholies'

– an interesting choice when the material on show within was all 'profane' in the sense of the word then understood. Look out for a version of Giotto's *Navicella* which was put in the Belvedere villa in the seventeenth century, possibly to decorate some kind of fountain or grotto, possibly accompanied by the famous classical statue nowadays usually called Ariadne, but then called Cleopatra. In the Pinacotheca, the picture gallery, you can find some of the paintings which once hung in St Peter's before getting the mosaic treatment. In the innumerable classical statues lining the walls of the Belvedere and the Museo Pio-Clementino you'll see where Canova got his aesthetic from.

Only some of the state apartments are reliably accessible to the public. But you will see several lightly or heavily disguised references to Old St Peter's: in the Nicholas V chapel by Fra Angelico; in Raphael's *Fire in the Borgo* in the Stanza dell'Incendio and (I've argued in the text) his *Dispute on the Blessed Sacrament* in the next-door Stanza della Segnatura, as well as Botticelli's *Sacrifice of Aaron* in the Sistine Chapel. Raphael also seems to have worked several references to New St Peter's into his designs for the row of offices or apartments known as the Stanze, even though it was still very much a pipe-dream when the paintings were executed. The backgrounds to *The School of Athens*, *The Expulsion of Heliodorus from the Temple*, *The Coronation of Charlemagne* and *The Mass at Bolsena* all seem to toy with designs made by Bramante, Peruzzi and Raphael himself.

Other more direct references to St Peter's are beyond public reach. Two frescoes in the Vatican library show Michelangelo's design: one half-finished and one in its projected, complete state. Some lovely frescoes by Paul and

Matthijs Bril in the Tower of the Winds and elsewhere bring out exactly the sort of dialogues between new buildings and ancient ruins that I've discussed in the text.

One last good thing about the Vatican museums is that normally you exit via the Scala Regia, so get to see Bernini's Constantine and the monumental entrance to the Vatican palace. You almost certainly won't get to see the frescoes in the Sala Regia, the grand stateroom at the top of the stairs, which among other subjects show Frederick Barbarossa preparing to bend the knee to the Pope in Venice, and Peter of Aragon seeking to be confirmed in his rulership of the Two Sicilies outside Old St Peter's.

St Peter's is so elaborately interwoven with its urban context that specifying buildings or viewpoints which might illuminate some aspect of it seems unduly restrictive. The 'approved' viewpoints for the church are discussed, or at least listed, in Chapter 7 above and elsewhere. But it keeps edging into one's sights all over Rome. One famous viewpoint is a keyhole in the Priory of the Knights of St John of Malta, Rhodes and Jerusalem, up on the Aventine hill.

As for other buildings, the Pantheon in Piazza Rotonda is crucially important (Pasquino is nearby, on Via Pasquino), as are the remains of the Basilica of Maxentius, on the southeast corner of the Forum near Via dei Fori Imperiali, and the Tempietto, in a cloister beside San Pietro in Montorio up on the Janiculum. Inside the main church are tombs by Della Porta and Bernini. The Tempietto is almost never open, but pleasing enough from the outside. A plaque by the north wall of the main church records how the Tempietto was 'miraculously unharmed' during the French bombardment of 1849 – another interesting parallel with St Paul's in London.

Distinctly unlike St Peter's to look at but intimately related to it by status and use is St John Lateran (Piazza San Giovanni in Laterano, metro San Giovanni). This embodies a different conservation philosophy from the Vatican basilica, retaining different phases in its construction side-by-side in a garish polyphony. Borromini's nave is a good example of his plastic, organic architecture (his patron, Virgilio Spada, wrote that 'he believed that Nature was the enemy of corners, and that animals, shaped by nature alone, never had them'). One curiosity in the cloister is the *sedia stercorata*. This is sometimes coyly rendered into English as the 'humble chair', but a better translation would be the 'shitty chair'. It is an antique throne decorated with Gothic pinnacles and Cosmati work, conventionally believed to be a latrine. Papal initiates had briefly to sit in it from the Middle Ages until, I would guess, 1870.

Inside the church, an ambitious reliquary which is said to contain bits of all the apostles stands in front of the apse. The delicate octagon of porphyry in the baptistery next door is a pretended memento of Constantine's alleged baptism by Sylvester.

To see more examples of Bernini's work, try the Cornaro Chapel in Santa Maria della Vittoria, on Largo Santa Susanna near the Acqua Felice, a few hundred metres on the city side of the Porta Pia. Further along Via XX Settembre is Bernini's church of San Andrea al Quirinale. Also good are the statue of the Blessed Ludovica Albertoni in San Francesco a Ripa in Trastevere (Piazza San Francesco d'Assisi), and the Chigi Chapel in Santa Maria del Popolo, just inside the Porta del Popolo on the northern edge of the city. This last was originally designed by Raphael as a kind of mini-St Peter's though his work is invisible now. It is the location for an episode of

Dan Brown's *Angels and Demons*, Bernini having apparently been one of the Illuminati, whoever they are. It also has a choir designed by Bramante, whom nobody has yet accused of belonging to any secret societies so far as I'm aware.

For other sites associated with the cult of St Peter, try the Mamertine prison on the northern tip of the Forum just behind the Vittoriale, the enormous 'wedding-cake' at the southern end of the Corso. This was turned into a church of sorts, but the custodians ask for a donation if you want to go in. San Pietro in Vincoli, just off Via degli Annibaldi, has the chains in which the apostle was supposedly bound; it also has all that remains of Michelangelo's Julius tomb. Outside Rome is the church of Domine Quo Vadis on the Via Appia Antica, a good place for a peaceful, if not exactly solitary, country walk if you're in Rome for a few days. The Roman tombs which line the street are mostly not well preserved, but they give plenty of atmosphere. The tomb of Cecilia Metella, around half an hour from the city walls, retains some of its travertine facing and some of its frieze reliefs; it's often depicted in topographical prints of the city, and so some-times participates in a dialogue of rhyming cylindrical forms with the Amphitheatrum Castrense, the Colosseum and the unfinished St Peter's. Also on the south side of the city, just next to Porta San Paolo in the Aurelian wall, is the Pyramid of Caius Cestius, by some accounts one of the two *metae* which mark the site of Peter's martyrdom. San Paolo fuori le Mura, heavily restored but once the partner of St Peter's, is a mile or so further south along Via Ostiense (metro Garbatella or San Paolo). EUR is reachable by metro and bus from the centre; SS. Peitro e Paolo keeps normal church hours, so don't aim to visit it in the middle of the day.

LIST OF ILLUSTRATIONS

ILLUSTRATION CREDITS

Library of Congress: 17, endpapers; Sir John Soane's
   Museum: 18

ACKNOWLEDGEMENTS

I would first like to thank the staff of the British Library, the Witt and Conway Libraries and Sir John Soane's Museum in London, and of the Archivio di Stato di Roma. A kind award from the Society of Authors enabled me to get to Rome for two research trips. The Ufficio Scavi at St Peter's smuggled me into an expertly-led guided tour of the Vatican Necropolis at short notice, and the Vatican press office helped me see the Pope in action on St Peter and St Paul's day 2006. Annabel Potter proved an excellent advisor on contemporary Roman politics and culture, not to mention contemporary Roman beachlife.

I'd also like to thank the staff of the Park Hotel, Amsterdam and the Hotel Aequa, Vico Equense   where more work on the book had to be done than I had foreseen   for letting me get under their feet.

For references, suggestions, quotations and thoughts I thank Mark Bostridge, Heather Ewing, Opher Mansour, Mark Payne, Douglas Pocock, Abigail Price and Rupert Shortt. For their wisdom and humanity during the editorial process, I thank Mary Beard, Peter Carson, Penny Daniel and Annie Lee; for expert Photoshopping, Katie Willmett; for bookchat and advice, David Miller.

For acts of patronage, advocacy and support both known

to them and unknown I thank Marielle Boyd-Hunt, Juliet Carey, the late Simon Carey, Paul Claydon, Lucy Dallas, Patricia Deasy, Lindsay Duguid, Will Eaves, Holly Eley, Pete Elston, Simon Grant, John Lloyd, Dominique Magada and Steve Cahill, Lydia Miller, Wena Miller, Angela Pertusini, Lucy Potter and Julian Clark, George Taylor, Anna Vaux and Frances Wilson.

INDEX

WONDERS OF THE WORLD

This is a small series of books that will focus on some of the world's most famous sites or monuments. Their names will be familiar to almost everyone: they have achieved iconic stature and are loaded with a fair amount of mythological baggage. These monuments have been the subject of many books over the centuries, but our aim, through the skill and stature of the writers, is to get something much more enlightening, stimulating, even controversial, than straightforward histories or guides. The series is under the general editorship of Mary Beard. Other titles in the series are:

Published
Mary Beard: **The Parthenon**
Simon Bradley: **St Pancras Station**
Cathy Gere: **The Tomb of Agamemnon**
Simon Goldhill: **The Temple of Jerusalem**
Keith Hopkins & Mary Beard: **The Colosseum**
Robert Irwin: **The Alhambra**
Richard Jenkyns: **Westminster Abbey**
John Ray: **The Rosetta Stone**
Gavin Stamp: **The Memorial to the Missing of the Somme**

Unpublished
Geremie Barmé & Bruce Doar: **The Forbidden City**
Iain Fenlon: **St Mark's Square**
Rosemary Hill: **Stonehenge**
Giles Tillotson: **Taj Mahal**
David Watkin: **The Roman Forum**